UNITY IN MID-CAREER

UNITY

AN ECUMENICAL CRITIQUE, EDITED

IN MID-CAREER

BY KEITH R. BRIDSTON AND WALTER D. WAGONER

The Macmillan Company, New York
Collier-Macmillan Limited, London

The Macmillan Company, New York
Collier-Macmillan Canada Ltd., Toronto, Ontario
DIVISIONS OF THE CROWELL-COLLIER PUBLISHING COMPANY

Library of Congress Catalog Card Number: 63-15050
Printed in the United States of America

CONTENTS

v

Section Three

THE GREAT DEBATE
ABOUT EMERGING CONCILIARISM

Section Four

UNITY AND THE
SOUND BARRIER

UNITY IN MID-CAREER

A LONG HARD LOOK

Keith R. Bridston and Walter D. Wagoner

Walter D. Wagoner, in attendance at both the New Delhi and Evanston Assemblies of the WCC, is a member of the Committee on Interpretation and Support for the US Conference of the WCC. A minister of the United Church of Christ, for the last eight years he has been Executive Director of the Fund for Theological Education, administering Rockefeller Fellowships.

Keith R. Bridston is an American Lutheran who has served on the staff of the Student Christian Movement of Great Britain and Ireland, was a secretary of the World's Student Christian Federation in Geneva, and a missionary in Indonesia, teaching in theological seminaries in Java and Sumatra. He was Executive Secretary of the Commission on Faith and Order of the WCC and is now Executive Director of the Lilly Endowment Study of Pre-Seminary Education.

Introductory Reflections

The tides of Christian unity, moving wave on wave, for more than fifty years have been mounting and deepening. No man-made dikes can or should long resist this surge which comes, we believe, from the movement of God's Holy Spirit. Dikes and dams still remain; indeed, there seems to be a small army devoted to raising up new ones, or at least sandbagging those that already exist. Nevertheless, we have confidence that the great spiritual tide of unity will prevail, however much it may be diverted or temporarily blocked by man's devices.

This does not mean that we see clearly the ultimate goals of unity that God intends for His Church. But one essential truth of the ecumenical movement is that together we seek to understand more fully the kind of unity to be sought and that together we resolve to be more responsive to the unifying impulses of the Holy Spirit in our various churches. This means that the attitudes of church members, the organizational structures of the churches themselves, the seminaries, the different councils of churches—the whole of ecclesiastical existence—must be kept under unremitting pressure to think about unity and to do something about it. For this concern is not something peripheral to the life of the churches. Christian unity is not a goal apart from the mission of the Church and the spread of the Gospel. It is not an idolatrous competitor to the central affirmations of the faith. It is a precondition for, as well as a result of, the faithful proclamation of the Good News to all men. In fact, the guilt we feel about disunity, as well as the energy we expend on the ecumenical movement, comes from the growing realization that the Gospel is crippled and broken by a divided Church.

The World Council of Churches is the center of many of the most poignant ecumenical hopes of our day. Those who are contributors to this volume have deep affection for it and are deeply committed to the cause which at the moment it uniquely embodies. The dreams and sacrifices which so many, from so many lands, have built into the World Council forbid any glib or debonair criticism. It is with that in mind that we are striving to say something that will strengthen the common cause and keep alive the common hopes.

Whether one considers the World Council to be an infant or an adolescent, its ambivalent character makes it imperative that it should be subjected to the free winds of open debate and the hard knocks of sharp criticism. Prolonged mothering and over-protection, in the aura of excitement surrounding its birth, may only delay the discovery both of what it is and of what it is called to do. For until the World Council comes to the self-realization of its own integrity as a manifestation of Christ's unity (however inadequate or provisional) it is in constant danger of becoming not a sign of hope of what the churches together might be and do, but a projection of what the churches now are and do separately. It is then not a proleptic token of the unity which God wills for His people but a forlorn extension of the willful division in which His people find themselves, and to which they are resigned.

This book, then, is presented in part as a contribution to the type of self-criticism in the spirit of candor which is necessary (if not welcomed or agreed with) in this stage of ecumenical development. To many of us it appears that the ecumenical movement, in and outside the WCC, is in danger of stalling "on dead center." We know how movements of reformation and renewal—not to speak of revolutions—cool and begin to jell. We know how much of Christian history has moved from "doxology through theology to sociology." Lava hardens. Or, to put it another way, men wish to build tabernacles on the Mounts of Transfiguration.

No realist, of course, can quarrel with the fact that ideas must take shape, and in taking shape in human society they must be organized. We do not deny this. On the contrary, it is precisely why we are concerned that the convictions and the faith which underlie the quest for unity should be objectified and institutionalized in such a way that they neither remain in mid-air like the smile without a cat in *Alice in Wonderland*, nor, on the other hand, become petrified prematurely in inappropriate institutional forms and organs. This book is offered as a modest contribution to that indispensable process of self-examination without which life is intolerable and through which growth and development may take place. It is, at the same time, an open invitation to others, equally committed to these principles, to join in the effort to rescue the "great new fact of our time" from premature senility.

We are thinking of some of the immediate challenges faced

by the World Council of Churches: how to move beyond structures and procedures too woodenly agendized, how to prevent
unity from being captured and domesticated by the churches;
how to maintain flexibility and openness to new developments
and new ideas; how to avoid introverted and esoteric clique-ism;
how to become institutionalized without ceasing to be a movement.

Pari passu, problems outside the limits of the WCC are becoming more clearly defined and the more we see of them as they
emerge the more formidable they appear: national and regional
isolation, unilateral confessional and denominational consolida-
tion, ethnic and cultural self-sufficiency. We are becoming aware
with a sense of increasing urgency of the demands which the
world is placing upon us as Christians for a relevant social
and political witness, for a common missionary strategy and
evangelistic proclamation, for a living exhibition of true human
community—all of which depend upon a wider and deeper and
more vital manifestation of Christian unity than the churches
in separation have yet been able to show forth.

This book, therefore, is not to be regarded as the petulant
whining of those who couldn't care less, or a negative attack by
those opposed to the ecumenical movement, nor even stereotyped
posturing by "angry young men." It is a collection of exercises
in committed criticism by those who agree that, matched against
the magnificence of the divine unity seen in Jesus Christ, there
must be a live, self-critical, programmatic, and unrelenting
movement dedicated to the vision of oneness and devoted to the
embodiment of it in word and in truth.

The essays which follow spell out some of the major problems, crises, and opportunities which now are before the ecumenical movement.

—East-West tensions, for instance, express themselves in
ways much stronger and more complex than Iron-Curtain clichés
suggest. Father Schmemann may startle many a Western
Protestant with his critique of the vast differences between
Eastern Orthodoxy and the Western constituency in the World

Council. Elisabeth Adler, from another angle, keenly diagnoses the cheap assumptions Christians in both East and West make about each other. And from yet another perspective, from Burma, U Kyaw Than balances the valid interests of ecumenical regionalism over against what is often a glib globalism.

—Another portentous issue is the type of conciliarism we desire and what authority we wish it to have. Ralph Hyslop, Walter Leibrecht, Lewis Mudge, and Henry Van Dusen argue different aspects of the problem and illustrate why many feel this issue is probably the most important and the most baffling of all the long-range ecumenical problems. Will the World Council of Churches, despite the self-imposed and oft reiterated restraints of its Toronto Statement, slowly become not only more churchly but more authoritarian? Should it? Has its own eagerness not to be or become a "super-church" inhibited it from fulfilling a role which even may free-churchmen would welcome for it?

—The constitutional structure and internal organization of the World Council is another perplexing problem. The New Delhi Assembly provoked long and hard thinking, both among the WCC's officialdom and those outside it, about the institutional form of the Council and its parliamentary operation. Some, including the editors of this volume, believe that serious mistakes have been made: in placing Faith and Order under the Division of Studies and thus subordinating the role of one of the major classical streams in the ecumenical movement; in making the Division of Ecumenical Action an organizational wastebasket; in keeping youth delegates at Assemblies segregated at a safe distance from parliamentary effectiveness; in failing to provide for office rotation policies (even the President of the United States is limited to two terms), especially for the General Secretariat and the Chairmanship of the Central Committee, even in the face of the remarkable abilities of the present incumbents. Liston Pope and Keith Bridston raise these and related issues, while not always agreeing on the remedies.

—Those not at New Delhi, so to speak, include the parish

minister from Tokyo and the milkman from Kansas City. What does it all amount to back at home? Who cares? Who understands? Is the ecumenical entourage only talking to itself? John Garrett, William Cate, Robert Paul are not lacking in candor as they make suggestions concerning the communication of the Gospel and ecumenical strategies related to its spread by news media, educational materials, parish programs, and work of councils of churches. Robert Tobias delineates the factors involved in formulating an ecumenical theology which will speak to all sorts and conditions of men.

—And what about the ecumenical training of ministers? Is theological education going on as though the ecumenical movement never happened and as though ecumenical commitment has no implications for congregational life? Walter Wagoner depicts the significance of the theological education of ministers for the effective implementation of Christian unity.

Had space permitted, attention might have been given to a greater variety of hopes and fears, issues and problems, before the World Council and the ecumenical movement as a whole.

For example, the role of national ecumenical agencies such as the United States Conference for the World Council of Churches needs thorough review. At present the US Conference, with due regard to the limitations imposed upon it by the Central Committee (including budgetary restrictions) is able to perform only a minimal program. Were it not for its capable staff, it would be able to do even less. But the drama of Christian unity, routine tasks and glorious vision alike, needs to be presented much more widely and vividly across the country. Younger leadership, both lay and clergy, needs to be identified, enlisted, and ecumenically engaged. Local ecumenical institutes ought to be fostered and strengthened. The US Conference, in particular, needs to be either coaxed or dragged screaming from the restricted and cloistered pattern of its work.

Protestant evangelical conservatism, as much as Roman Catholicism, must be encouraged to enter the ecumenical circle, talked with and prayed with. While great communions such as the Southern Baptist and the Missouri Lutherans and major Pentecostal bodies remain on the periphery of the ecumenical movement it lacks some of the main marks of catholicity for which it strives. This whole dimension of ecumenical relations needs further attention.

Finally, there is no specific essay by a Roman Catholic vis-à-vis the ecumenical movement. The tide of books on Protestant-Roman Catholic dialogue, plus the pomp, circumstance, and publicity surrounding the Vatican Council, give some excuse for omitting this crucial topic at this time, though Ralph Hyslop's essay is grounded in a survey of Roman Catholic conciliarism, and the contributions of other authors obviously bear upon it both directly and indirectly.

In conclusion, we believe that, for all the omissions and for all the limitations, the intent behind the essays is significant. Religious organizations and leaders, unlike those on the political and social stage, tend to be treated with cloyed deference. In terms of public criticism they are often given a "clergy discount." The WCC is no different, except that it is even further separated from the public sand-paper by its very prestige and novelty—the suffused romantic glamour surrounding it inhibits frank talk and earthly thoughts. The long road ahead for the WCC, and other ecumenical agencies, ought to be traversed, not like the Ark of the Covenant in holy untouchability, but as in the rough-and-tumble of our all too human pilgrimage, where sharp criticism and good-humored loyalty rub shoulders.

THE WORLD COUNCIL OF CHURCHES
AS OPPORTUNITY AND PROBLEM

THE WORLD COUNCIL OF CHURCHES: UNCERTAIN SAMARITAN

Liston Pope

Liston Pope, Professor of Social Ethics at Yale Divinity School, as well as its former Dean, served on both the Central and Executive Committees of the WCC between the Evanston and New Delhi Assemblies. His analysis of the organization of the WCC evidences his warmhearted concern for the ecumenical movement as well as his training as a critical sociologist.

THOUGH it is a small organization in terms of such institutional factors as staff and budget—smaller even than a great many parishes or local councils of churches—the World Council of Churches is a complex body, and discussion of its internal structure may best proceed in terms of several distinct though interrelated levels of operation.

Membership

The fundamental membership roster of the World Council consists of denominations (201 of them since New Delhi), ordinarily referred to inside the organization as "member churches." National councils of churches or national Christian councils may become "associated" with the Council or "affiliated" with its Division of Christian Mission and Evangelism, but there must be

11

prior consultation with the member churches. Individuals are often brought in as advisers or consultants at various levels of operation, but approval by the individual's denomination is a prerequisite. Even nominees for membership on the Central Committee or for a position on the staff must be cleared with their respective churches. Though the programs and pronouncements of the Council generally assume a worldwide aspect, there is no question that the center of authority and power lies in the various denominations.

In view of the minimal requirements for membership (made slightly more stringent at New Delhi), it is rather remarkable that the World Council manages to function or even to survive. Its member bodies have little in common theologically, all told, except a confession of "the Lord Jesus Christ as God and Saviour," and even this central affirmation is subject to diverse interpretations. They exhibit nearly the full spectrum to be found in non-Roman Christendom in respect to polity, liturgy, theology, sacramentalism, ordination of the priesthood, and other ecclesiological matters. Among them are to be found churches associated with nearly all the political, cultural, and ethnic traditions in a divided and pluralistic world. The sociologist who presumes that a common culture or ethos must underlie effective institutional integration would be puzzled by the World Council. How can the Pentecostals and the Eastern Orthodox sit down together, or march together? Or the Russians and the Americans? In its membership the Council does transcend most theological and social boundaries; whether it can convert or transform them is another question.

It is rather a paradox that an organization devoted primarily to church unity should have as its constituent members a large number of denominations devoted to their own self-preservation. The profession of a desire for greater church unity is widespread among these denominations, of course, and there are many evidences that the desire is real rather than feigned. Certainly the member churches have demonstrated their intention to have closer contact with one another and to engage in common action in a number of ways. But neither they nor the World Council has been willing to become very specific as to what "unity" finally implies or requires. The Council's own disavowal of any intention to become a superchurch is genuine and self-preservative, but it does not meet the issue. Is the World Council's role that of the drone who dies after the queen bee has been fertilized? If so, well enough—but how is the predominance of one queen bee over the other contenders to be established?

Whatever the content of its message, communication by the World Council to its member churches is voluminous, though the problem of reaching the *membership* of the churches remains a difficult one, varying by countries, languages, and denominations. But the response of the churches to the positions, study documents, and inquiries issued by the Council is the weakest link in the ecumenical chain of contact. Only about one-quarter of the member churches acceded to the request of the Evanston Assembly that they "report to the Central Committee in due course as to the results of the study and action undertaken" with regard to the Section Reports adopted at that Assembly, though the Reports were distributed widely.

On a matter so specific as the proposed integration of the World Council of Churches and the International Missionary Council, the requested response from member churches and councils of the respective bodies was remarkably uneven. As of the terminal date set for replies, two-thirds of the member councils of the IMC had been heard from; at the same date about half of the member churches of the WCC had voiced an opinion. It is obvious that a committee of the Church of Scotland was understating the position when it observed that "much thought and experiment are needed both as regards disseminating the results of ecumenical thinking and as regards reporting to ecumenical headquarters." The World Council has learned to speak and to act, often with point and power. But its constituency has not learned to talk back in a satisfactory and stimulating way.

The Assembly

The Assembly, as the supreme legislative body for the World
Council's own activities, is the logical forum for expression of
the views of member churches, and it has fulfilled that function
at least to the point of requiring strict limitation on the length
of speeches from the floor! The body is a rather large and unwieldy one (there were 1,006 official participants at New Delhi,
with 577 voting delegates, as compared with 2,320 persons
registered in all official categories at Evanston), and it meets
only once in each six or seven years, for a period of approximately three weeks. Though it is reported that the meeting at
New Delhi was more largely a "working body" than a spectacle
to be observed by delegates and public alike (as at Evanston),
there was still serious question at New Delhi as to the competence of the Assembly for all the business brought to it.
Inevitably, authority tends to be delegated to the Central Committee, and then to the Executive Committee (which theoretically
can take only "provisional decisions" with regard to questions
of policy), and then by the Executive to "its officers and the
General Secretariat." There is far greater centralization of responsibility for decisions than the freewheeling discussion at the
Assembly, or even at the Central Committee, would suggest.

Certain thorny questions are involved in the organization of
the Assembly. Voting delegates are selected by the constituent
churches, but the Executive Committee or Central Committee
may suggest on occasion that particular individuals would be
highly desirable as officers of sections or committees and might
well be given some kind of official status. Every member church
is entitled to at least one voting delegate; most members avail
themselves of this opportunity, though a few find it necessary to
decline for financial reasons. With a ceiling of 600 delegates
(700 for the next Assembly) for the meeting at New Delhi, with
latitude of 20 percent, more or less, just under one-third of the
places had to be reserved for the minimum representation of the
member churches.

Naturally, a certain amount of haggling has been and will be inevitable as to the distribution of the remaining seats. The Constitution of the Council provides that due regard shall be given "to such factors as numerical size (of the respective churches), adequate confessional representation and adequate geographical distribution," and that approximately one-third of the delegates shall be lay persons. Since few churches with a single delegate are likely to appoint a layman, nearly half of the additional places are theoretically intended for lay men or women, further increasing the competition for clerical places.

Bargaining for seats is generally conducted in an irenic spirit, and it is prompted by diverse motives: the desire to have one's own traditions represented adequately, or at least as adequately as other traditions; the effort by members of the Central Committee (which alocates seats) to demonstrate to their constituencies that they have been "on the job"; the desirability of having representation from churches in Asia, Africa, and Latin America out of all proportion to their percentage of total membership; and so forth. As in many other aspects of the life of the World Council, however, the "calculus of the ecumenical spirit" leads to rather odd results. To use comparisons most familiar to churchmen in the United States, representation at New Delhi per 1,000 claimed church members was more than twice as high for the American Lutheran Church as for the United Lutheran Church, and more than six times as high for the American Baptist Convention as for the National Baptist Convention, Inc., a Negro denomination. And it is interesting that only 16 representatives of the Russian Orthodox Church were present (though it had just been admitted to membership), when it claims the allegiance of perhaps fifty million persons, in comparison with the 27 delegates allotted to the Methodist Church in the USA with about ten million members. It is little wonder that the Eastern Orthodox churches, with their sprawling if somewhat undefined membership, sometimes raise questions about the adequacy of their representation at the various levels of World Council activity. It is time to raise the question

as to whether the principles of allocation ought not themselves
to be enlarged or refined. Certainly every member church must
be entitled to one delegate. One proposal has suggested that
further representation should be related in some way to taxation
—that is, to the amount of financial support given by a member
church to the work of the Council. This formula is dubious in
principle, would be extremely difficult of application, and almost
certainly would have no chance for adoption.

Voting on most questions before the Assembly is by delegates
rather than by member churches as such. If this procedure is to
be retained, it may be in order to ask if the World Council should
not consider changes in its fundamental structure of membership, perhaps basing itself on world confessional bodies or
national councils of churches—entities already related to it in
rather ambiguous ways. This reorientation would probably bring
more problems than it would solve.

Or the Council might adopt the practice of the United Nations and allow each member church to have only one official
vote on all or certain types of questions before an Assembly, as
is the case now in voting on the admission of new members. Each
church could have present, in addition, as many advisers to the
official delegate as accommodations, financial resources, or other
conditions would permit. This scheme would give far greater
weight, of course, to the votes of the smaller churches, and
would allow them actually to be decisive if they acted in concert.

It is unlikely that any formula for representation can be
found that will entirely transcend impulses toward influence or
power. Religious societies are hardly less liable to such impulses
than secular ones. As the "rules of debate" adopted by the
World Council recently recognize, however, the validity of
churchly proclamations is not established by the counting of
heads. In retrospect, the likelihood of the Second Coming or the
necessity of the conversion of the Jews is probably not much
affected by actions taken at Evanston.

The question as to responsibilty for preparations for an
Assembly, involving choice of site, main theme (if any), organi-

zation of discussion and business, preparation of materials, and the like, also needs fresh consideration. The Third Assembly at New Delhi was planned entirely by the normal committees and departments of the World Council, and especially by the Central Committee. Earlier assemblies had been preceded by special preparatory commissions, but for New Delhi only a special Committee on the Message was added to the regular machinery, plus the various committees in India to prepare local hospitality. It is in order to raise the question whether preparations for the Assembly required a disproportionate amount of time and energy of the regular instrumentalities of the Council, and whether this procedure also tended to centralize control over the Council still further. The Central Committee did not select the delegates to the Assembly, but it planned nearly everything else in advance, as was its duty under the plan adopted. Perhaps the Committee would have been wiser to appoint a knowledgeable preparatory commission quite independent of itself.

The Central Committee

Meeting annually except for rare exceptions, the Central Committee of the World Council is really the chief policy-making agency of the organization. It may not take decisions inconsistent with the policies adopted by the previous Assembly, but those policies were themselves suggested for the most part by the previous Central Committee.

With 100 members, the Central Committee is a group of manageable size. It can easily be lodged in any number of places in the world, and is thereby incomparably more mobile geographically than the Assembly. Of more importance, the Committee is small enough to allow active participation by its members with regard to all matters that come before it. Its meetings by design seek to combine theological discussion and administrative decisions; important questions of doctrine or polity generally evoke more heated discussion than does consideration of the annual budget.

The problem of "balanced representation" in the membership

of the Committee does not appear to be a grave one, especially
in view of the provision that any member church not represented
on the Committee may send a representative to its meetings, with
voice but without vote. Several questions might be raised, however, about the distribution of membership in other than confessional or denominational terms. The new Committee elected at
New Delhi contains only sixteen laymen—half the percentage
suggested for membership in the Assembly. Of the sixteen only
five are women, though at least half of the church members in
Christendom must be of the female sex. The USA has the largest
contingent, with 21 members, as compared to 9 from the United
Kingdom, 6 from India, 5 from Russia, and 1 from the Far East.
There have been complaints that Asia, Africa, and Latin America have not been represented adequately, and this complaint
may be justified from the standpoint of world perspectives,
thought not from that of the distribution of church members
among the continents.

A deliberate effort is made to combine continuity and rotation of representation in the membership of the Committee. Of
the persons elected at New Delhi, 21 are from churches not represented on the previous roster. But 32 persons were carried
over from that roster, and it is in this group that the center of
influence and leadership will undoubtedly lie. As a matter of
fact, the deliberations and decisions of the Central Committee
are guided very largely, intentionally or otherwise, by a fairly
small group of its members, most of whom have been incumbents
since the meeting of the First Assembly at Amsterdam in 1948.
Unless special pains are taken to prevent it, the Committee
could easily become a gerontocracy—a fate that has been the
peril of several other world organizations in the past.

The Executive Committee

The Executive Committee (composed of 12 members plus
its officers before New Delhi, 14 members since then) is unques-
tionably the nonstaff center of authority in the World Council.
Meeting twice a year, it is ostensibly an administrative body

dealing definitively with questions of organization and personnel. But as the executive agent of the larger Central Committee
it is far more than a financial clerk or personnel foreman; it has
decisive influence on nearly every aspect of program planning,
theological posture, and ecumenical relations.

In part because of the substantial demand on the time of its
members, the Executive Committee is composed very largely of
denominational executives, whose schedules, if always under
heavy demand, are somewhat more adjustable than those of the
average pastor, layman, or theological professor. Between
Evanston and New Delhi 9 of the 14 members were full-time
denominational officers. As one veteran member of the Committee
put it, "If I were not in this meeting I would be in some other,
and I would rather be here." All but two members of the committee before New Delhi were clergymen with theological training, but the two laymen were among the ablest theologians in
the group. The clergymen voiced some uneasiness as to whether
they really were "theologians"; perhaps their ambivalence at
this point helps to explain the occasional introduction of "theological" considerations even into the discussion of proposed
budgets.

As a smaller group than any other volunteer agency of the
World Council, the Executive Committee is also the most mobile.
Questions of total expense and competing obligations have not
deterred it from ranging widely over the world in its meetings.
In recent years, for example, it has held sessions in Australia
and Buenos Aires, though more meetings have been held in
Geneva than anywhere else. By the same token, the Committee
has been used frequently as an entourage of evangelistic out-
riders for the World Council, with a strenuous program of public meetings for its members before and after its official sessions.
In Australia there were so many public occasions, with thousands of people in the audiences, that one member finally described the Committee as "Visser t' Hooft's Touring Troupe."
The ringmaster was no less active than his performers.

As may be desirable, there is ordinarily little change in the membership of the Executive Committee between meetings of the General Assembly, though its personnel is selected annually by the Central Committee. At this one crucial point the principle of "balanced representation" is somewhat abrogated, with individuals being chosen more largely for their own abilities than as representatives of a denomination or region. For most of the period between Evanston and New Delhi the Committee consisted (with its officers but not the Presidium) of five Americans, two Britishers, three Asians, one African, and four continental Europeans. Even so, all the principal confessional traditions were represented.

The Executive Committee has taken its work very seriously. At times its members have not had full access to information about matters of grave import, but perhaps certain delicate questions should best be reserved for disposition by its officers or the Secretariat. At the same time, the Committee has not been simply a rubber stamp for staff recommendations. Nor has it been a self-protecting private club; its small size and frequency of meetings have permitted its members to become good friends, but on occasion there have been sharp disagreements among them. For the most part its debates have been a model of interconfessional and international frankness and charity.

Membership on the Executive Committee provides the best illustration of the levy, physically, emotionally, and timewise, on the volunteer leaders of the World Council. Members of the employed staff set a worthy example of self-expenditure. But most of the World Council's volunteer leaders, and especially the members of the Executive and Central Committees, have primary and demanding jobs in their own denominations, probably also in their national councils of churches and in the world confessional bodies, and in many other contexts. To use a fine phrase by Truman Douglass, they are the "ecumenical Rover Boys," and the price of their tickets cannot be counted in money alone. There is no need to mention their obligations to their families or local communities, as they are seldom to be found in such limited circles. It is little wonder that the wife of one ecumaniac, herself a gently bred Southern lady accustomed to epithets only against Yankees, has referred to the World Council for years as "the damworldcouncil." It is not possible, of course, to prove that the ecumenical die young, because the principal ecumenists are seldom young.

A study of the desirable pattern of meetings of the Executive and Central Committees during the period between the Third and Fourth Assemblies was authorized in 1959, and the *ad hoc* committee, composed mostly of staff members, recommended in the following year that no substantial changes be made. One of the chief arguments was that the bureaucratic tendencies incipient in any organization would be intensified if there were less frequent checks on staff and program by volunteer representatives of the churches. This argument is partly specious: the volunteer committees are primarily review agencies rather than initiatory bodies, so far as the work of the staff is concerned, and in effect they most often afford a sanction for the bureaucracy that already exists. It is regarded on all sides as rather bad form for a member of the Executive or Central Committee to probe deeply into the internal operations of a department of the Council, or to raise questions that might be embarrassing. Rather, these committees spend their own initiative on interchurch relations and on documents dealing with general policy— in short, on the vaster issues that confront the Church, while bureaucratic (and highly competent) staff work goes merrily or grimly along.

Divisions and Departments

The meetings of the Assembly, and to lesser degree of the Executive and Central Committees, provide the glamorous occasions in the life of the World Council. An occasional special consultation helps to focus attention on some issue of wide import—an *ad hoc* conference on migration, or on the plight of Arab refugees in the Middle East, or on the relation of the churches in South Africa to racial questions. But the day-to-day work of the World Council is carried on by staff members in the various divisions and departments of the Council; each of these has its own volunteer advisory committee, but the staff members are responsible for most of the operations. The table of organization has hardly changed in the last eight years, but a notable dissatisfaction with the existing organizational pattern became evident at New Delhi, and a fresh study of the internal structure of the Council was authorized for the immediate future.

No attempt at a systematic description or evaluation of the work of the various departments is appropriate for this volume, which is intended to be critical and stimulating rather than analytical. A few random observations, mostly critical in character, may be in order, against a background of admiration for the dedication and industry manifested by the staff of the Council in nearly all of its undertakings.

The focus of the Division of Interchurch Aid, Refugee and World Service (as it was unhappily renamed at New Delhi) is far from clear, especially with regard to its relation to the new Division of World Mission and Evangelism. Its works of mercy for refugees since World War II have become legendary, but now the Division, having been given a mandate for permanent operations on a worldwide scale, seems to be rather confused as to its objectives. Its own budget, drawn mostly from the benevolence funds of member churches, is nearly twice as large as the operating budget of the World Council itself, as seems appropriate. Its focus on refugees has been somewhat dimmed, at least theoretically, in favor of attention to more fundamental schemes of reconstruction in various parts of the world. But the content of its schemes is somewhat elusive, and the ability of the World Council to make an important contribution alongside other voluntary, governmental, and United Nations programs is open to question. The Good Samaritan is staggering a bit on the road to Jericho.

No brief statement could do justice to the work of the Commission of the Churches on International Affairs. Its work has been outstanding in relation to the United Nations, and it has been invaluable in the formulation of policies with regard to such questions as nuclear testing, disarmament, religious liberty, and the population explosion. On occasion it has been criticized for failure to take more definitive positions, but the commission has genuinely undertaken to achieve world perspectives that transcend particular ideologies or political barriers. The World Council itself has had a certain amount of influence on the actions of nations; it is noteworthy that secular governments and heads of states have gone out of their way, perhaps with a certain wistfulness, to extend hospitality to the Central Committee and to the successive assemblies.

The Division of Studies cannot decide whether it is a discussion leader, a pamphleteer, or a research scholar. In recent years it has sponsored a far-flung study on the role of the churches in areas of rapid social change; this activity has undoubtedly helped a great many churches and churchmen to assess their resources and their turbulent environments more accurately, but it has added very little to knowledge about the plight and opportunities of churches in underdeveloped areas. Its projection of studies for the next period—the finality of Christ in an age of universal history, Biblical and historical thought about religious liberty, the training of the ministry, the Christian witness to peace—does not comprise a coherent or exciting prospectus. Most of these important topics could be handled more competently by a single scholar in the solitude of his study than by a commission with a staff and budget.

Recent pressure for improved status and resources for the Faith and Order Department illuminates many of the organizational problems of the World Council. As one of the two main streams that merged in the Council, the Faith and Order movement envisaged a considerable degree of continuing autonomy and prestige, but now it finds itself reduced to the status of one department among several in the Division of Studies. The tail that wagged the dog was clipped at Evanston, and the creature has become increasingly unhappy with its small rudder.

The situation is rendered more difficult by the fact that the

Faith and Order Department addresses itself to one of the central and most embarrassing problems of the World Council: what does church unity really require? By the same token, what is the proper role and status of the Faith and Order movement? Is it still a movement, or an item on the table of organization? In either case, what is it supposed to do? It is generally agreed that the comparative method of analyzing ecclesiology and doctrine has gone far enough; the problems of church union are now *understood* well enough, and the urgent necessity is that they be *attacked*. Often supposed to be interestingly academic, the Faith and Order enterprise is now suspected of seeking to become activistic and to do something about unity rather than merely to talk about it. But its espousal of the unity of "all in each place" leaves its adherents on the hinterland of intelligibility.

The Faith and Order Department is undoubtedly moving from consideration of church unity in general to concern for churchly unity in particular. In a rather perverse sense, the goal of Faith and Order might be interpreted as the abolition of the World Council through the realization of organic rather than conciliar unity. Realization of any such goal appears to be extremely remote. As a way station, the World Council may or may not hinder progress toward that destination. Apparently the Assembly at New Delhi was ready to approve much stronger efforts of the Secretariat toward unity across racial and ethnic lines than toward unity across confessional lines.

The Division of Ecumenical Action has always been a grab-all; whatever was left over was put there. Its constituent units have nevertheless often been inventive. Ecumenical work camps have lifted the horizons for thousands of young people. The laity have been somewhat assuaged (by the way, who are the laity in Protestantism?). The Department on Cooperation of Men and Women has tried to shift the emphasis from feminism to a more objective basis, and now has a new and important mandate for concern with family life. The Ecumenical Institute and Graduate School at Bossey have been an ornament with a staff of high quality, even though its attendants have often resembled the Protestant equivalent of Roman Catholic tourists stimulated to a pilgrimage.

The Department of Information needs a larger and more aggressive staff to do its wide-ranging job most effectively. The World Council and its associated enterprises have glamour and newsworthiness, as the representation of the press, television, and other media of communication at Evanston and New Delhi has attested. But the ecumenical movement has hidden its light under a bushel, and has been little more than a candle in the dark of the world, in a time when Telestar and its successors may further universalize communications. The Council's publicity displays and scrapbooks should not deceive it into thinking that it has had very much impact on the total life of the churches, to say nothing of the wider affairs of man.

The integration of the International Missionary Council and the World Council of Churches, with the consequent creation within the latter of a Division of World Mission and Evangelism, raises many questions. Will the missionary impulse be thereby more largely institutionalized and circumscribed? Or, as has been piously hoped, will the concern for the mission of the Church permeate more deeply into all the other concerns of the World Council? The fate of the Faith and Order movement in this respect is not encouraging; once an autonomous and vigorous force, this movement is now a small department of the Council, subject to the internal pressures and rivalries of any organization—and to the budget.

The Staff

Extensive discussion of the staffing problems of the World Council is neither necessary nor desirable at this point. As measured against responsibilities and opportunities, the employed staff is remarkably small—not to be compared in size, for example, with the staff of the National Council of the Churches of Christ in the USA. But the productivity of the World Council staff is amazing; if all the conferences, trips, pamphlets, and study guides engineered from 17 route de Malagnou, Geneva, were to be placed end to end, the most indefatigable ecumenical voyager would be dismayed. One member of the Executive Committee complained that he needed a full-time file clerk to keep up with materials coming from the World Council alone.

Obtainment of a competent staff is often a rather haphazard and difficult business, especially with regard to the secretaryships of the various departments. The Executive Committee's subcommittee on personnel must try to find, let us say, an Anglican from outside Britain whose church officials would be willing to release him from the important job that he is doing in order that he might teach at Bossey for a three-year period for two-thirds of his present salary. Possibilities for "advancement" are negligible, as are the prospects of a really good salary. For years its salary scales have been an embarrassment to the World Council, even in comparison to rates prevailing in Geneva—though assurances were given at New Delhi that some improvement is in prospect. Even plans for retirement income, under development for several years, have been slow in maturing; part of the problem lies in the fact of rapid turnover in the staff, but this is by no means an excuse for an inadequate pension arrangement.

Apparently the morale of the employed staff is very high, owing in part perhaps to its own cosmopolitanism and also to the sense of having a part in a pioneering venture. When the staff moves into its shining new headquarters and begins to have a sense of permanence, a quite different mood may come to prevail. The World Council needs to face up, and soon, to the fact that it has a bureaucracy and that the problems of personnel and salaries must be faced realistically. Stars in the eyes are no permanent substitute for money in the bank.

Bureaucracy or not, the staff of the Council has kept itself remarkably fresh and flexible. Its members talk with one another a great deal—their professional equipment might include a vial of Dobell's solution in addition to entero-vioforme. But they have developed very little jargon—far less, for example, than did the leaders of the religious education movement in the

United States, or the social gospel movement. Their chief fault may be the assumption that important questions can best be solved by a commission or conference.

The World Council faces a change in its top professional leadership in the next few years. In the past it has drawn heavily on the Student Christian Movement and comparable sources for its executives. As it comes of age it may need to think more specifically, for the next generation, about scholars and diplomats.

Financial Support

A religious organization tends to gloss over financial problems, just as it tends to mask power drives. Such questions, as the Committee on Programme and Finance put it, are of "a worldly character."

The financial operations of the World Council have been handled with great skill, but one may question whether the basis of its support is fundamentally equitable or sound. Nearly all of the funds for the annual operating budget come from contributions by or through the member churches. In the fiscal year 1954 the churches in the USA contributed 76 percent of the total, though they comprised only 20 percent of the members.

American delegates to bodies of the World Council have not used this situation in an effort to increase their own influence in deliberations of the Council; to the contrary, they have tried almost pathetically to ignore the Council's utter reliance on financial support from the United States. But the situation is still an extremely unhealthy one, and is further compounded by a similar disparity with regard to special gifts to the Council for refugee work, a new headquarters, study projects, housing at the Ecumenical Institute, or whatever. Delegates from other countries have refrained on occasion from vigorous comment on proposals for new programs (to the distress of their American colleagues) because of the presumption that the American churches would have to pay the bill.

Admittedly the question of contributions from member

churches is a complex and difficult one. Sources of funds for the churches themselves vary greatly; the American concept of voluntary stewardship by members of the churches is only beginning to be understood in a great many countries. There can be no doubt as to vast differences among the churches in "ability to pay."

Whatever the difficulties, the existing imbalance has unfortunate effects inside the Council itself and also exposes the entire organization to the charge that it is a vehicle of the West in general and of the United States in particular. The charge is not warranted, and the recent admission of new members from Russia, Eastern Europe, and Africa may help to belie it. Meanwhile, more rigorous efforts should be made to attain greater financial parity. Should the American churches go so far as deliberately to reduce the percentage of their contributions to the operating budget of the World Council, while maintaining or even increasing their support of the total ecumenical enterprise? Probably not, as this kind of unilateral action would represent a form of domination not revealed hitherto.

The Future

The future of the World Council of Churches depends to large degree on developments in the secular world beyond its control. The gates of hell may not prevail against the Church, but all hell can break out in and around the World Council. Its new headquarters buildings in Geneva can be vaporized in the same blast that demolishes the old League of Nations building nearby. Like the League, the World Council can also crumble from within by failure to meet effectively the tasks placed before it, and especially the task of visible and organic unity in the Church.

The World Council tends to err toward either routine repetition or toward a mild frenzy. On the one hand there are too many meetings, too many consultations, too many trips, too many teas and receptions, too many documents. Commissions or the staff write background papers for the various committees;

the committees meet and read and ratify and rewrite the same statements in paraphrase. Members of the Executive Committee in particular reread essentially the same documents so often that they come to know them by heart.

On the other hand there is too little evidence of individual reflection and imagination and dissent. In his report at New Delhi the gifted chairman of the Central Committee, Franklin C. Fry, observed that "the World Council has never experienced a really calm day since it came into existence." That's too bad, even if hyperbole.

Perhaps the World Council is imperiled most of all by its own respectability and success thus far. Its meetings are comprised of a congeries of archbishops, bishops, deans, theological professors, denominational executives, and that poor token little woman and an occasional cuff-pulling local pastor. To use Toynbee's phrase, it needs "an internally seceded proletariat," willing to be not petulant but awkward and disputatious. The ecumenical smile needs to be complemented by a furrowed brow and a hard jaw.

The second generation of volunteer ecumenical leaders very largely passed off the stage at New Delhi. Will a new leadership, possessed of charismatic power combined with administrative skill (can these be combined?) emerge in time to promote ecumenical *movement* rather than merely to preserve an ecumenical organization?

The principal power in the internal organization of the World Council is the strange and compelling work of the Holy Spirit. As one reads the records of the successive Assemblies, the reports from divisions and departments, the eloquent speeches and the pointed resolutions, few sparks fly up from the eternal anvil. But there is a spirit breathing through all these records and through the human implements by which they have been produced. It is this intangible Spirit, whispering through the assemblies and between the lines of the documents, but not subject to depiction on any table of organization, that gives an ineffable quality to an admittedly imperfect agency.

DOMESTICATING THE REVOLUTION

Keith R. Bridston

The World Council of Churches as Institution and Movement

In St. Andrews, Scotland in 1960 the Central Committee of the World Council of Churches concluded a three-year discussion on the "Future of Faith and Order" with the decision to leave Faith and Order as one of the subordinate departments of one of the major divisions of the Council. To the outside observer it must have seemed strange that the "future" of one of the two founding movements of the World Council should have been in question at all, and certainly inexplicable why one of the major streams of ecumenical history should find such a precarious institutional channel in the Council so soon after its founding. At the Amsterdam Assembly in 1948 Dr. W. A. Visser 't Hooft in his Report Presented on Behalf of the Provisional Committee said: "Faith and Order represents the oldest and most basic of all activities for which the Council is asked to accept responsibility. It stands at the beginning and at the end. . . . Its work is less conspicuous than that of other departments, for it must proceed quietly and patiently. It will therefore need a considerable amount of autonomy within the total structure."

The explanation offered by one of the Faith and Order veterans to this strange contradiction was the Bismarckian comment: "Politics is the art of the possible." However it may be explained, the Faith and Order debate vividly illustrated the difficult transitional stage the ecumenical movement has entered through the formation of the World Council of Churches: a movement is becoming institutionalized. Indeed, the dialectic between movement and institution is perhaps *the* characteristic mark of the life of the World Council in this second decade of its existence. And the controversy over the proper place of Faith and Order within it, whatever else may be said about it, had the beneficial, if accidental, effect of shaking many out of the complacent assumption that the World Council was just the old ecumenical movement in a new guise. It was revealed with almost startling clarity the extent to which the Council was an established and conservative ecclesiastical institution. The Faith and Order veteran's use of the word "politics" in summarizing the long and often rough debate was apt. For though the whole review was initiated with assurances of a free discussion, the actual concrete decisions were finally made more on the basis of expediency than on ideological merit. What presented itself as an unparalleled opportunity for a comprehensive reappraisal of the nature, purpose, function, and form of the Council was prematurely aborted by pressures which arbitrarily resolved the theoretical issues by power politics. The practical structural consequences which the Faith and Order group had drawn from its analysis of the present ecumenical situation and the general theological principles underlying the ecumenical movement touched too close to the organizational nerve of the existing power structure. Too many highly placed officials felt threatened by proposals involving organizational change. Too many officeholders and prospective candidates were running for election or reelection as the New Delhi Assembly loomed large on the political horizon to risk institutional realignment. And so the Faith and Order organizational proposals were unceremoniously, though sanctimoniously, scuttled. The art of the possible had been exercised.

Of course, this is not a new story. It is as old as the Church itself which, as we know from its annals going back to the New Testament period, has always exhibited both misery and glory in its life. What may be difficult for this ecumenical generation to realize is that this ambivalence is inevitable in such an ecclesiastical institution as the World Council of Churches too. Those who took part in the ecumenical movement in its pre-World Council days, when it was primarily a voluntary association of those sharing a common vision of the ecumenical reality of the Church, naturally saw the World Council as both the culmination and ultimate embodiment of that movement and tended to take it for granted that this "new and unprecedented" (as the Toronto Statement puts it) entity was the fulfillment of the radical and prophetic tradition of the movement as a pioneering and renewing power among the churches. It was almost inevitable, against this background, that the difficulty of dynamically harmonizing the classical tension between church establishment and charismatic movement in this new body would be underestimated.

That the original period of enthusiastic euphoria is now giving way, especially among the younger generation, to critical reappraisal is, therefore, only to be expected. In fact, it is essential. For the future of the ecumenical movement in the coming period may well rest upon the ability of its new leadership to put aside the rose-tinted spectacles (with their romantic aberrations) of their predecessors and to look at the World Council of Churches, and the problems of ecumenical institutionalization it epitomizes, with clear and coldly realistic eyes. In particular, there must be the utmost clarity about the tension between institution and movement now embodied in the World Council and the potentialities both destructive and creative which that tension contains.

On the positive side, the institutionalization of the ecumenical movement in the World Council of Churches is a mark of success. It means that the member churches have formally committed themselves to the ecumenical cause. The World Council is the institutional token of the Amsterdam covenant of the churches' intention "to stay together." But this new, comprehensive ecumenical institution is at the same time a potential threat to further ecumenical movement, and that for two main reasons.

In the first place, the World Council is a potential hindrance to ecumenical movement simply because it is an institution. Modern sociologists have begun scientifically to scrutinize institutional ecology and behavior. For instance, Kenneth Boulding in *The Organizational Revolution* outlines certain "iron laws" of organization which suggest the almost irresistible influence of oligarchical, hierarchical, and monopolistic forces in institutional evolution. Whatever else may be said about the ecclesiological nature of the World Council, it is still an institution and it will, in large measure, be and act like other institutions. Thus, though it may be impossible to predict with any degree of certainty what the ecclesiastical future of the Council may be, it is reasonably certain that it will show the characteristic marks of general institutional existence in the intervening period. One of the marks is conservatism. The natural tendency of an institution is to remain at rest, to stay where it is, to be immobile. In brief, an institution resists change, and movement means change. This, in a nutshell, is the dilemma posed by the World Council of Churches' institutional "success" for continuing ecumenical movement.

In the second place, the World Council of Churches is a potential barrier to ecumenical movement because it is not only an institution but an ecclesiastical institution. A good deal of thought has been devoted to the ecclesiological significance of the World Council of Churches. But the almost obsessive fear evidenced in the Toronto Statement of 1950 that the World Council might be considered a "superchurch" may obscure a greater danger. With a certain degree of cynicism one might say that the self-interest of the member churches is probably

an adequate safeguard against overt ecclesiastical pretensions
on the part of the Council. A more real and much more subtle
danger, however, is that the World Council might become a
"superorganization"—a kind of ecclesiastical monstrosity which
could well exhibit some of the worst attributes of corporate
ecclesiastical life without ever being a "superchurch" or even
pretending to be churchlike.

History is, of course, replete with vivid examples of ecclesiastical sins and the fact that the World Council is not a church,
much less a "superchurch," does not make it less susceptible to
the traditional failings of ecclesiastical bodies. It may not evidence the more parochial and pedestrian limitations of local
congregations, but there is certainly no guarantee that it will
not manifest those of classical Christianity as time goes on.
Nicolas Berdyaev has written of the Ecumenical Councils that
"few things are more expressive of human pettiness, treachery,
and fraud." The World Council need not descend to this level,
but the fact that it does not technically fit the definition of
"church" will not prevent it from doing so. In short, the fact
the World Council is not properly "church" does not give it a
natural immunity against common ecclesiastical afflictions. It
is just more susceptible to some than to others.

To take one example, ecclesiastical bodies are subject to
the special temptation of bolstering their structures, programs,
and procedures with theological rationales. Their ordinary
institutional behavior is given spiritual sanction. And so the
status quo is defended, not on its own merits, which might well
justify this conservatism, but as an order which somehow expresses the will of God. The Programme and Finance Report
presented to the New Delhi Assembly in 1961 is a current ecumenical illustration of how the World Council itself may slip into
this classical ecclesiastical trap of theologically rationalizing
the establishment and thus in effect blocking new ecumenical movement. Bertrand Russell has written that "to an organization which has ideal ends, and therefore an excuse for love
of power, a reputation for superior virtue is dangerous, and is

sure, in the long run, to produce superiority only in unscrupulous ruthlessness. The Church preached contempt for the things of this world, and in so doing acquired dominion over monarchs." (*Power*, 49). Here again, the World Council has not descended to these depths of institutional depravity, but church history is a constant warning to it that it should not become complacent about its potentialities for showing the signs of traditional ecclesiastical self-deception about its own institutional existence.

Bearing in mind these potential hindrances to ecumenical movement which the World Council embodies in itself through its character as an ecclesiastical institution, can it as such a body actually be a means of ecumenical movement? The answer, it seems to me, is yes. But only under certain conditions.

The first condition is that constitutionally the World Council should be considered basically and primarily a vehicle of movement. Its organizational structure and constitutional form should be of such a sort that it facilitates rather than hinders movement. Needless to say, the Council by being "of the Churches" necessarily represents institutionally the ecumenical *status quo*: the Council by its constitutional limitations is what the churches are now. But the Council is also the extension of the ecumenical movement, the vanguard of where the churches are to go. When the Council was first formed the question was raised as to whether the tradition of its parent bodies in drawing upon the contributions of those having "the special gifts of prophetic vision and discernment which are required for the building of the ecumenical fellowship and the passing on of its witness" was not endangered by the constitutional principle of putting the Council exclusively under the control of the "chosen representatives" of the churches. On the whole, the World Council has shown a healthy mixture of the official and representative elements and the spontaneous and unofficial initiatives in its life and activities. But as the Council is further removed from the original voluntary leadership of the movements which preceded it and becomes more formalized in its structure and procedures, it is urgent that the current tendency to absolutize the representative principle should be thoroughly reviewed.

The second condition is that the procedural life of the Council should provide for movement. Or to put it another way, since politics is an inevitable concomitant of institutional life, including ecclesiastical life, it is important that there should be a good political tradition: that is, a politics in which those striving for conservation of the *status quo* and those for movement and change have equal rights and privileges.

The debate over the future of Faith and Order, already referred to, as well as the election of officers and committee members at New Delhi, exposed the existence of an "establishment" within the Council, an "in-group", to use sociological parlance, which in fact controls the Council and ultimately determines its policies.

This can be illustrated in several ways. The Assembly, the ultimate parliamentary authority of the Council, is so large and unwieldy, has such infrequent meetings, and confronts such an overwhelming agenda, that it is almost completely ineffective as a political instrument. It has become, as critics of both Evanston and New Delhi have pointed out, an ecumenical spectacle rather than a responsible policy-making body and is in effect, as one New Delhi delegate reported to his constituency, controlled by the secretariat—"the steel hand under the velvet glove."

The Central Committee, which in theory exercises the political functions the Assembly is unable to handle, has its own serious limitations. For one thing, it is not fully representative of the membership of the Council. Being a selective group, a determinative factor in its political effectiveness—and freedom —is the means of its selection. In practice, the Central Committee is handpicked by the General Secretary with the advice and approval of the officers and the Executive Committee. The Assembly, as New Delhi showed, has very limited possibilities for either veto or initiative in regard to the Central Committee membership. The result is that the Central Committee can become a "kept" body, politically indebted to the very persons and groups which it is intended to control.

The Executive Committee, which theoretically represents the Central Committee and constitutionally at least could have a regular turnover of members, has developed into a self-perpetuating "in-group," the hard core of the ecumenical establishment along with the Geneva secretariat. Though it is obvious that this power center is precariously remote from the scrutiny and control of the member churches, there could be a healthy political dialectic based on a division of powers between the Executive Committee and the secretariat. The trouble is that the relationship is organizationally incestuous. Over a period of time so many political debts and favors are accumulated between the secretariat and the Executive that the free exercise of the latter's powers are sharply curtailed, particularly on issues involving the inner organization of the Council itself, as in the Faith and Order debate.

And the end result is that the powers of the Council's secretariat are much greater than any organizational diagram might suggest. One of the problems of limiting these powers is that the secretariat itself is not rationally organized and the power structure within it is not constitutionally recognized. An illuminating sidelight on this was provided during the course of the debate on the future of Faith and Order at St. Andrews in 1960. There had been rumors that a so-called "triumvirate" of the secretariat (representing policy, administration, and finance) had vetoed the proposal to give Faith and Order divisional status. Whatever the validity of these speculations, the existence of a hierarchical control center in the secretariat was verified in the "compromise" put forward which allocated a place on the "Staff Executive Group" (made up of the General Secretariat and the directors of the Information and Finance Departments) to the Director of Faith and Order.

The importance of this concession was somewhat lost on the Central Committee since, ironically enough, it had never been formally notified of the existence of the "SEG" and had little conception of its strategic significance in the Geneva staff operation. The very fact that this solution was put forward as a serious alternative to a divisional reorganization was the first indication for many Central Committee members of the actual power of this nonconstitutional secretarial cabinet—a body whose political potential no one who has served on the World Council's staff underestimates and whose policies no staff member challenges with impunity.

In other words, the institutional structure and the political dynamics of the World Council are far more complicated than the already intricate organizational charts of the Council would intimate, as has been said, and the danger is (as with any other political organism) that the constitutional forms become totally divorced from the political realities of it. It has been said that the Faith and Order proposals for structural change were effectively blocked by the opposition of the General Secretariat, who made the issue in effect a vote of confidence: "Any arrangement opposed by the General Secretary can only be a paper victory" as one ecumenical veteran put it at St. Andrews. The proper role of a General Secretary is, of course, itself a fascinating institutional problem (as the analogy of the United Nations indicates): should, for example, the General Secretary, in view of his strategic political position, be (unlike a British Prime Minister, for instance) so remote from the control of an electorate? But the point is that, powerful as he may be, even the General Secretary can often only articulate the policies of the establishment and not infrequently must be its scapegoat as well, especially when the establishment chooses to remain hidden. And this, of course, is sure to become more acute when a new General Secretary is appointed, for he, unlike his predecessor, is likely to be the nominee of the establishment, its man, and perhaps picked out for precisely those qualities which make him a passive and malleable tool in its hands. This may not happen. But it certainly could. And the wider constituency of the World Council and all those concerned for the ecumenical movement as a whole should be aware of it.

In any case, the question remains: how can the World Council, even if it does not pretend to be a "democratic" body, be subjected to the initiatory and veto powers of its membership and not be absolutely controlled by a small, self-perpetuating executive clique, or an oligarchical secretariat?

The Faith and Order case illustrated some of the current weaknesses of the World Council as a political organism. It showed the power of an establishment to block actions it does not approve. It showed that many of the key elective officers of the Council are actually dependent on the goodwill and support of the General Secretariat rather than upon the will of the Assembly representing the member churches—whatever its theoretical constitutional powers may be. It showed that key committees for examining and reviewing the operations of the Council (for instance, the Programme and Finance Committee) are inadvertently put in the position of dealing with controversial issues which involve its members in a conflict of interests; they are asked to decide on matters in which their own institutional future is at stake, an almost unthinkable situation in the realm of "dirty" secular politics.

Without party, Disraeli once said, parliamentary government is impossible. Lacking a party system, through which secular politics is disciplined, how can church politics and in particular the politics of an ecumenical organization such as the World Council be placed on a rational and systematic basis. Like secular politics, church politics must come to terms with and incorporate the facts of power, of divergent views, of ideological diversity, of conflicts of interest, in systematic forms and procedures. The Toronto Statement dealt with the *nature* of the World Council. A comparable statement is found in the Programme and Finance Report on its *task*. What is needed now is a substantial definition of its *form*. Because the Council is the result of movement and is intended as the continuing instrument of movement, a definition of the form best lending itself to the fulfillment of these ends is indispensable. It may be hoped that the proposals of the Programme and Finance Committee "to set up the necessary machinery for the reexamination of the organizational pattern" between the Third and Fourth Assemblies "to the end that the structure of the WCC may be more adequate to its true, and unfolding, task" may soon be implemented. Such a group must face the question of whether the political instrumentalities it now possesses are adequate to bear the stress that continued ecumenical movement places upon them and will place upon them and, in particular, whether they are sufficient to bear the burdens of the pressures of self-interest on a personal level and power struggle on the institutional level that are the inevitable concomitants of movement which is organizationally embodied.

The idea of ecumenical politics may be abhorrent to many, but chiefly to those with docetic illusions about ecclesiastical existence. The only real alternative to politics is bureaucratic domination; as Karl Mannheim has pointed out in *Ideology and Utopia:* "The fundamental tendency of all bureaucratic thought is to turn all problems of politics into problems of administration . . . in every revolution the bureaucracy tries to find a remedy by means of arbitrary decrees rather than to meet the political situation on its own grounds." The only way in which the procedural life of the Council can be a channel for ecumenical movement is that it become politically rationalized and not bureaucratically controlled. Edmund Burke at the end of the eighteenth century said: "The science of constructing a commonwealth or renovating it or reforming it, is like every other experimental science, not to be taught *a priori.* Nor is it a short experience that can instruct us in that practical science." (*Reflections on the Revolution in France*). The experience of the World Council is short, but that is also what makes it an exciting and hopeful sign of ecumenical progress and hope.

Finally, in order for the World Council to be an instrument of movement, its *provisional* character needs to be constantly kept in mind. From 1938 to 1948 the WCC was "in process of formation." But that process does not end there. To be true to the ultimate ecumenical goals the World Council can never

be an end in itself. An institution is, in a certain sense, the end
of movement. But it may also be the means of further movement,
movement which its very institutional character makes possible.
As the Council becomes settled in the steel and concrete of
permanent headquarters after moving out of its "tents" and as
it accumulates the routinized procedures of institutional establishment, its provisional character may be forgotten. As time
passes, the provisional may be mistaken for the final.

The strongest protection against this is the cultivation of
a spirit of provisional expectancy among all those active in
ecumenical work, but particularly among those responsible for
leadership of ecumenical organizations. It is natural and under-
standable that those deeply committed to an organization and
intimately connected with its direction should sometimes fall
victim to a kind of innocent naïveté about their importance in
determining the destinies of that body and, as a result, are not
sufficiently sensitive to the forces (including themselves) which
are tending to absolutize that which is, and must be, provisional.
In their concern for conserving the tradition of the past, in
maintaining continuity, they are inclined to try to nail down
the future. They are tempted to dictate what the "process of
formation" should bring forth. They are moved to be masters
of a continuing reformation, rather than subjects of it.

The election of officers and committee members of the World
Council at the New Delhi Assembly has raised concern in many
quarters in this connection. Certainly the perpetuation of the
ancien régime among the officers and members of the key policy-
making committees was not motivated by ruthless concern for
self-perpetuation. It was, in fact, argued that this continuity
was necessary in view of the anticipated resignation of the
General Secretary in the period before the next Assembly. But
might not the same arguments be used to justify similar actions
in the future? In short, the principle of being "in process of
formation" needs constant translation into concrete political
realities. The breaking of the previous tradition that the officers
of the Central Committee should not succeed themselves by

the reelection of the incumbents was undoubtedly justifiable in terms of the qualifications of the candidates. But what about the political principle involved? In one of the preparatory documents for the Assembly Dr. Franklin Fry speaks of the World Council looking forward to its own demise. And it is exactly on those grounds that perpetuation of such a large group of officers and committee members might be legitimately questioned. For the principle of having a regular and substantial turnover of leadership in the Council is argued, not on a lack of confidence in any particular group of persons, but on the confidence that the Council is sufficiently strong and stable to be able to survive and even profit by the periodic infusion of new blood into its organizational arteries. If it is a provisional institution it must be prepared to live provisionally.

As has been said, the World Council is subject to the same institutional forces as other institutions. Seymour M. Lipset in his introduction to Robert Michels' *Political Parties* observes: "Political parties, trade unions, and all other large organizations tend to develop a bureaucratic structure, that is, a system of rational (predictable) organization, hierarchically organized. . . . But the price of increased bureaucracy is the concentration of power at the top and the lessening of influence by rank and file members. The leaders possess many resources which give them an almost unsurmountable advantage over members who try to change policies." Or as Michels himself puts it: "Large-scale organizations give their officers a near monopoly of power."

The World Council of Churches derives much more of its dynamism than is generally recognized from the movements which preceded. Those movements, particularly the Student Christian Movement, were marked by their independence from the ecclesiastical establishments, their character as voluntary associations, their simplicity of organization and operation, their lay constituency, and, not least, their youthful leadership. Of course, the World Council cannot be the Student Christian Movement "writ large" (though it is sometimes thought to be). It is a foregone conclusion that the World Council with its size and prestige and ecclesiastical dignity is going to be led by an over-sixties generation and, however much they may try, they inevitably lack the spirit of heretical nonconformity, the mood of restless experimentation, the willingness (and ability) to risk failures, the passion for change, that are the indelible seals of youth and which were the marks of the leadership of the pre-World Council ecumenical era.

It may be assumed that the creative and renewing forces which gained expression through the Student Christian Movement and the other ecumenical movements which preceded the World Council are still at work. But what will happen to them if the World Council succumbs to what Camus has called the "Caesarian revolution," wherein the original revolutionary dreams and ideals are "renounced in favor of the bitter morality of the empire-builders"? This is the challenge of the ecumenical movement to a new generation of leadership. Radical criticism of present ecumenical institutions such as the World Council may be thought by some in the establishment to be "troublemaking." But unless this is allowed, and even encouraged, the results could be tragic. What we need, as George Bernard Shaw put it in his Preface to *St. Joan,* is "to bear in mind that unless there is a large liberty to shock conventional people, and a well informed sense of the value of originality, individuality, and eccentricity, the result will be apparent stagnation covering a repression of evolutionary forces which will eventually explode with extravagant and probably destructive violence."

It is well to remember this ecumenical history, though probably unwise to become nostalgic and sentimental about it. Most golden ages are more glittering in retrospect than in reality. In any case, the future of the World Council as an institution of the ecumenical movement depends in some measure on a memory of this past, but applied to the realities of the present. Ecumenical participation requires the spirit of self-discipline and self-abnegation based on the faith that God is at work within

the movement and its institutions and a confidence that the
future is in God's hands and not ours. It demands an honesty
about our facility in deceiving ourselves about our motivations
and aspirations regarding its welfare and destiny.

And what should never be forgotten is that the World
Council of Churches is part of a reforming movement.
But it can be an effective part only insofar as it is itself
constantly open to reformation. The Council may not give in
to all, or even to any one, of the institutional forces within it
which are ever pushing it to be more monolithic than polylithic,
more rigid than flexible, more stratified than homogenous, more
conservative than radical, more hierarchical than democratic.
But the forces are there and these centripetal and oligarchical
pressures must be curbed and checked constantly from within
by its constitutional structure, by its political operations, and
by the common spirit of all its participants to renounce self for
the common good and for the building up of the whole body. As
Trevor-Roper has succinctly put it: "To reform is a frus-
trating task; to be reformed is maddening."

STRESS AND STRAIN
FROM EAST AND WEST

MOMENT OF TRUTH FOR ORTHODOXY

Alexander Schmemann

Alexander Schmemann, an Orthodox priest, is a professor in
St. Vladimir's Academy in New York. He was a delegate at
the North American Faith and Order Conference at Oberlin
in 1957. As a theological teacher in France, and later in the
United States, he has been one of the most articulate and
incisive spokesmen for Orthodoxy in the ecumenical movement.

*I*F the participation of the Orthodox churches in the Ecumenical Movement or, more precisely, in the World Council of
Churches, were to be evaluated on the sole basis of official reports, declarations, and statistics, there could be no doubts as
to the positive and optimistic character of such an evaluation.
Officially this participation has been indeed steadily growing
since the pioneering days of Stockholm and Lausanne and by
now virtually all Orthodox Churches have joined the World
Council. The image and place of Orthodoxy in the Council is
symbolized by the traditional election of an Orthodox hierarch
as one of the Council's five presidents. Orthodoxy—such seems
to be the significance of this symbol—is not only *in,* but it is
given actual leadership, is to become one of the *guiding* forces
of the whole Ecumenical Movement. *Officially* the Orthodox
participation in the WCC looks like a well established tradition, raising no question or doubts.

But does this official optimism correspond to the real situation? To this question I must quite honestly give a negative answer and my purpose in this brief essay is to substantiate it, that is, to show, first, that there exists a discrepancy between the official Orthodox position in the WCC and the "real" Orthodoxy, and, second, that this discrepancy constitutes an urgent issue for the WCC which, if it is not understood on time, may sooner or later lead to a major ecumenical crisis.

No one who has followed ecumenical developments from within the Orthodox Church would deny that, in spite of all official pronouncements, affirmations, and actions, the Orthodox participation in the WCC not only remains an ever open question but encounters a deeply rooted suspicion and even hostility that cannot be simply ascribed to dead conservatism, lack of interest, or mere provincialism. The suspicion is widely spread not only among laity but also among hierarchy and theologians. There exists, to be sure, an official position endorsed by Orthodox leadership. But a Western reader should be warned immediately that in the Orthodox Church "officialdom" cannot be simply identified with the voice of the Church. History is here to remind us that no official pronouncement is of any binding effect unless it is accepted by the whole body of the Church, even if it is very difficult, if not impossible, to give a clearcut definition of how such acceptance is to be achieved and expressed. What, for example, could have been more "official" than the unions with Rome signed at Florence in 1438 and in Brest-Litovsk in 1594? Yet neither was accepted by the Church and their failure only increased the number of tragic misunderstandings that make our present relations with Rome so difficult.

Today—as was the case then—the "official" position seems to me to be dangerously cut off from not so much the feelings or reactions of the "average" Orthodox, but from Orthodox *reality* itself, that is, the totality of spiritual, theological, and liturgical experience which alone can give life and authenticity to the acts of ecclesiastical policy. Yet the Orthodox partici-

pation in the WCC remains precisely on the level of "ecclesiastical policy" despite the very fruitful work performed by Orthodox theologians. For if participation means, above all, a real
sense of involvement and responsibility, an irrevocable certitude
of belonging, a kind of self-identification with the Ecumenical
Movement in all its complexity, achievements, and difficulties,
then one must openly admit that although Orthodox representatives may be *in,* the Orthodox Church as a whole is certainly
out. Representation here has not yet been transformed into
participation. The question is—why?

II

The Ecumenical Movement is by its very nature an encounter, a conversation, an accepted partnership in the search
for Christian unity and "wholeness." The encounter, however,
is fruitful and meaningful when it is founded on some degree
of mutual understanding, on a common language, even if this
language serves as a means of a sharp controversy.

The tragedy of Orthodoxy is that from the very beginning
of its ecumenical participation no such common language, no
theological "continuity" existed between her and her Western
partners, within, at least, the organized and institutionally
structured Ecumenical Movement. *There was no real encounter.*
For, as I will try to show, even the seemingly successful participation of Orthodox theologians and "ecumenists" was limited
and somewhat initiated by an artificial theological framework
imposed on it, and this not because of any bad will but by the
very nature of the early Ecumenical Movement.

III

To explain this initial failure, two facts are of paramount
importance. One is the multisecular *isolation* of the Orthodox
Church from the Christian West, the other a specifically *Western* character and ethos of the Ecumenical Movement.

It is indeed impossible to understand the uniqueness of the
Orthodox ecumenical situation without realizing that for many

*

centuries the Orthodox East was virtually absent from the life of the West, took no part in it, and, what is equally important, was not considered a part of it. This means that the crucial events in the Western spiritual and theological history—the Reformation and the Counter-Reformation, events which precisely shaped and conditioned the religious situation and the theological mentality of the contemporary Christian West, had minimal impact on the Orthodox Church and were not significant events of her own history and life. Isolated from the West and its religious effervescence, on the one hand, she was, on the other hand, forced into a kind of defensive immobilism by the external conditions of her own existence: the Turkish domination and its various consequences. And thus she remained basically unaltered in her structure, spirituality, liturgy, in the whole of her tradition. The only notable exception was the rather deep "westernization" of Orthodox theology, but it was an exception, confirming the rule. For, precisely because of its alienation from the traditional sources and methods, this "westernizing" theology, failing to have any significant impact on the life of the Church, was not really *accepted.*

It is this Eastern isolation of the Orthodox Church and her very real identity with tradition as formulated and accepted *before* the Western schism, that explain those basic presuppositions, which conditioned the initial Orthodox attitudes and reactions in the Ecumenical Movement and determined the subsequent development of Orthodox participation. To understand them in all their implications is of the greatest importance for all those preoccupied with the ecumenical future.

The first of these presuppositions concerns the very *orientation* of the Ecumenical Movement. If for a Western Christian, because of his historical background, the central ecumenical problem of Unity, Division, Reunion is formulated mainly in terms of the Catholic-Protestant dichotomy and opposition, for the Orthodox Church the fundamental opposition is that between the East and the West, understood as two spiritual and theological "trends" or "worlds" and it is this opposition that,

in the Orthodox mind, should determine the initial framework
of the ecumenical encounter. We must not forget that the only
division or schism, which the Orthodox Church remembers to
speak of *existentially* as an event of her own past is precisely
the alienation from her of the whole West. For at the time of the
fateful rupture between Constantinople and Rome (1054)
the latter represented both institutionally and theologically the
whole Christian West and it was as a whole that the West broke
its communion with the East. This, according to the Orthodox
point of view, was owing to an initial deviation from the common tradition, a deviation that blinded the West and made it
accept doctrines incompatible with the teachings of the undivided Church. Reformation, in this Orthodox perspective, was
understood as a crisis *within* the more general Western distortion of Orthodoxy, as a specifically Western development,
attributable to Western conditions and presuppositions. Therefore, the first ecumenical question, the starting point of the
whole ecumenical movement from the Orthodox standpoint, is:
What happened between the East and the West, when and how
did this alienation begin, what is its real scope and content?
There had to be, in other terms, a revaluation of the past, of
that history which at a certain moment ceased to be the common history for both halves of the original Christendom. The
Ecumenical Movement, to be fruitful and meaningful, had to
accept as its first item of investigation that initial and determining tragedy of the universal Church.

The second presupposition is the logical consequence of the
first one. It concerned the basic *terms of reference* of the ecumenical encounter and conversation. From the Orthodox point of
view the only really common language, the only workable set of
references in such a conversation could be supplied by that
tradition which at one time was accepted by all Christians, as
the common and universal teaching of the Church and that was
precisely the tradition represented by Orthodoxy. For again
it is to be remembered that at the time of the Western Schism
the *Eastern* tradition—that of the Fathers, Ecumenical Coun-

cils, and the *lex orandi* still formed the common basis and were thought of as not the "Eastern" expression of the Christian faith, as something specifically Eastern and, therefore, particular, but as indeed the universal tradition of the Church. It could therefore—if such was the Orthodox ecumenical thinking—give the ecumenical encounter a real framework of common references, a possibility to clarify the fundamental issues. Alien to the acute Western controversies and frustrations, the Orthodox Church could contribute, at least in her own eyes, a *tertium datum*, not as *her* tradition, but as a common heritage in which everyone can discover the starting point of his own spiritual and theological development.

Hence, and this is the third presupposition, the only adequate *ecumenical method* from the Orthodox point of view, was that of a total and direct doctrinal confrontation with, as its inescapable and logical conclusion, the acceptance of truth and the rejection of error. Throughout all its history Orthodoxy knew only those two categories: the right belief (Orthodoxy) and the heresy, without any possibility of compromise between them. Heresy was looked at as not so much as intellectual distortion, but as a deficient faith, endangering salvation itself. It is, therefore, truth, and not unity, which in the Orthodox opinion and experience had to be the real goal of the Ecumenical Movement; unity in this experience being nothing else but the natural consequence of truth, its fruit and blessing.

IV

None of these presuppositions had been accepted or even understood in the Ecumenical Movement when the Orthodox Church made its appearance in it. This means that from its very beginning the Ecumenical Movement was heavily dominated by Western religious and theological problems.

Thus, if the Orthodox understood the ecumenical phenomenon as encounter between the East and the West considered as the two "halves" of the original Christian world, the very sting of being just a "half" was almost completely alien to the West,

Protestant as well as Roman. The long isolation of Orthodoxy, on the one hand, the dramatic dynamics of its own religious history, developed in the West a sense of self-sufficiency which hardly left any room for the archaic and static "Easterners" who, only a few decades before, were an object of Western missionary proselytism. For the Christian West the ever-present and ever-burning tragedy was not its alienation from the East, but the collapse of its own religious unity in the crisis of Reformation and Counter-Reformation.

The Orthodox idea of an early and universal tradition as a common heritage and, therefore, a possible common ground for the ecumenical encounter was ignored, for there developed in the West another tradition: that of a polemical defensive and offensive theology in which the very concept of "tradition" was radically altered. For the Orthodox Church tradition is the living experience of the Church, existing prior to its formulation and definitions and independently of them. But the West reduced it progressively to an almost juridical category of *authority*, so that it is no longer the *content*, but the very *existence* of tradition that became the ecumenical problem and preoccupation.

And, finally, the central Orthodox affirmation that truth and truth alone is to constitute the formal "object" of the Ecumenical Movement, as being both the content and the form of unity, was also to be misunderstood and practically ignored because, in the Western experience, truth is understood primarily as again a formal "authority" and is therefore, opposed not to error, but to freedom. The very categories of "Orthodoxy" and "heresy" had here a connotation very different from the one they had in the Orthodox mind. And if in the Orthodox understanding, the ecumenical movement was to be centered on an ultimate choice between truth and heresy, the Western presupposition of it was that ultimately all "choices" are to be integrated into one synthesis, in which all are mutually enriching and complementary one to another. *The word "heresy," in*

*fact, is absent even today from the ecumenical vocabulary, and
does not exist even as a possibility.*

V

The initial misunderstanding which I have briefly analyzed
results, in my opinion, in a *fundamentally false position* of the
Orthodox Church in the WCC. It is false both theologically and
institutionally, and this falsehood explains the constant Orthodox "agony" in the Ecumenical Movement, the anxiety and the
doubts it raises in Orthodox consciousness.

On the theological level the Orthodox Church, because she
failed to impose her own vision on the Ecumenical Movement, her
own ecumenical presuppositions, had to accept and, in fact,
accepted its formulation in terms of the Catholic-Protestant
dichotomy. This meant not only that she was somehow forced
to identify herself with one of the two opposing Western positions, but also that she had to make her own all the derived
dichotomies: word, and sacrament, vertical and horizontal,
authority and freedom, and so on, typical of the Western theological situation, but fundamentally alien to the real Orthodox
tradition. In the absence of Rome, she was assigned the role
of the ecumenically acceptable Catholicism at the extreme right
wing of the whole spectrum of Protestant denominations. It is
indeed tragic that the Orthodox theologians and "representatives," with a very few exceptions, so easily accepted this assignment—accepted, perhaps without realizing it, a part in a
Western controversy; whereas their real contribution might
have been the overcoming of the Western impasses and wrong
dichotomies! It is here, probably, that the long "Westernization" of the Orthodox professional theology produced its negative fruit. For if it is true that the Orthodox Church is
hierarchical, sacramental, traditional, "horizontal," dogmatical,
Catholic, and so forth, neither of these "notes" or characteris-
tics simply coincides with the Eastern approach to them, be it
their affirmation and defense by the Roman Catholics or their
negation and criticism by the Protestants. Orthodoxy cannot

be simply reduced to the "Orthodox doctrine" of apostolic succession, seven sacraments, three degrees of hierarchy, and it is
even doubtful whether such "doctrines" exist in a clearly defined
form. Many of these terms themselves have been borrowed
directly from Western manuals and are to be still evaluated
in the light of the total and genuine Orthodox tradition. Yet
it was precisely as a "position" on this or that question that
Orthodoxy was always "presented" and "represented" in the
ecumenical conversation, but virtually never as a totality, as a
living spiritual reality which alone gives life and meaning to
its external forms. And then this position itself was usually
identified with an existing Western category which only enforced
the accepted theological framework. The "separate Orthodox
statements" attached to the reports of virtually all major
ecumenical conferences is a good, if too often a helpless, illustration of the feeling of being in a false position, which was
almost always that of the Orthodox delegates.

VI

But it is on the *institutional* level that the falsehood of the
Orthodox position within the WCC is the most apparent. Because of the Western religious situation, no other structure of
the Council was conceivable but the one based on the "denominational" principle. Since no common definition of the "Church"
is to be found, any group with some degree of organizational
autonomy must be accepted as "Church" even if this term does
not belong to its self-determination. This principle adequately
reflects the Protestant view of the Ecumenical Movement, but is
radically incompatible with those of either the Roman or the
Orthodox Churches. What is involved here is not a question of
prestige (The Orthodox Church being equal in "importance"
with some minor "denomination") but a question of ecumenical
truth and reality. For the division between Protestant "denominations" is radically different in its very nature from the division
between Orthodoxy and Protestantism, on the one hand, Orthodoxy and Roman Catholicism on the other hand. In the first

case there are disagreements within a basic agreement, in the second there may be partial agreement but within a radical disagreement, made painfully obvious by the impossibility of "intercommunion."

The ecumenical reality is threefold: Catholic, Protestant, Orthodox—but this is not *expressed* in the institutional forms of the Ecumenical Movement. Here again the blame is not with the Protestant architects of the WCC, who tried their best to incorporate in their own way the basic ecumenical tensions in the structure of the WCC (cf. the Toronto document) but with the Orthodox themselves who by accepting the "denominational" principle and applying it to themselves betrayed once more their own ecumenical mission and function: that of representing the wholly different "pole" of the experience of the Church, or, in other terms, the *Church* herself in all her reality and unity. This, however, is to be achieved not by the routine repetition of her claim to be the "true" Church but by the firm affirmation of the simple fact that in any ecumenical encounter the Orthodox Church is always and by her very nature the other "half" standing together *with*, and yet always *against*, the totality of the Protestants. And as long as this real opposition is not expressed in the very structure of the WCC, the position of Orthodoxy in it will be misleading and confusing for both the Orthodox themselves and their Protestant brothers.

VII

It is my hope that these remarks, sharp and disappointing as they may seem, will be understood as coming from a very real concern for the future of the Ecumenical Movement and the Orthodox participation in it. We have reached, it seems to me, the "moment of truth," and there is a great need for clarity and responsibility. So much has been given to us in the ecumenical encounter, so many wonderful possibilities open. We have no right to betray them.

EAST OF NEW DELHI:
REGIONALISM OR CENTRALISM?

U Kyaw Than

U Kyaw Than, a Baptist from Burma, was a lecturer in history at the University of Rangoon before joining the staff of the World's Student Christian Federation. He was responsible for the preparatory work leading up to the formation of the East Asia Christian Conference and is now its Associate General Secretary and a member of the WCC's secretariat.

O_{NE} can imagine the irony of a situation where a youngish Western churchman introduced to an audience a hoary ecclesiastic from Asia as a "younger churchman" from one of the newer nations! Yet it is the way most of the churchmen from Asia are regarded by those in the West, and only a limited number of the alert among them realize that there are in Asia churches such as those along the coast of Malabar in India which trace their history back to the apostolic days, long before Columbus discovered America or England first heard the Gospel. More recently Asia has come not only to be referred to as the area of the "younger churches" but also as that of the "new nations." It is no wonder that on occasion some Indians and Chinese (to take only the obvious and the glaring examples) have insinuated rather sarcastically about the preoccupation of the West with the history of just a few centuries while Asians think in terms of millenia.

Some fifty church bodies which at present make up the East Asia Christian Conference are found in countries of such a part of the world, each in its special historical setting and social environment so diverse from one another that it defies any kind of neat generalization. Militarist republicanism, socialist democracy, communism—all make up the variety of political environments in which these churches are found today. Being in a part of the world which is acknowledged by all as the home of the majority of world religions, these churches in Asian countries have also to take into account in their Christian witness the Hindu, Buddhist, Moslem, Shintoist, or Confucian systems of life in which their respective societies have been immersed for ages. In terms of numbers, the birthrate alone of countries such as China, India, or Japan defies any complacent hope ever to win them all for Christ. In spite of the disproportion between the total populations and the size of membership of the churches in these lands, there is cause for joy and gratitude to God for the fact of the existence of these churches in Asia. Among the some fifty church bodies which make up the East Asia Christian Conference, a number of them are small numerically speaking; some, though counted as one member, are in actuality federations of churches (for example, the Federation of Lutheran Churches in India which is made up of ten Lutheran church bodies), while some others such as the Batak Protestant Church in Sumatra and the Presbyterian Church in Korea have just between the two of them about one and a quarter million members.

The Isolation of Asian Churches

Dr. R. B. Manikam (now Bishop of Tranquebar), as joint East Asia Secretary of the World Council of Churches and the then International Missionary Council, used to emphasize how the churches in East Asia were lamentably isolated from one another in the past and that each of them knew more about the church in the far Western countries from where the missionaries had come to her rather than about the fellow churches in Asian countries. After calling of the World Missionary Conferences at Jerusalem in 1928 and at Tambaram in 1938, Asian churchmen began more and more to be thrown together. With that development in new patterns of contacts came also the discovery by these Asian churchmen of the similarity of the political and missionary situation of their own churches in their various countries. Three things arose out of these international and ecumenical encounters in world missionary conferences:

1. Inspiration derived out of a vision of world Christianity;
2. Desire for closer fellowship and cooperation with those fellow Christians struggling in the same missionary situation in neighboring lands;
3. Dissatisfaction with the fragmentation of the small Christian churches in Asia because of the emphasis on differences of church traditions as developed outside Asia.

The development of world Christian bodies drew them out of their isolation and placed them in the midst of a fellowship which extended around the world. As far as they were concerned there was no need for convincing them about the inadequacy and even the invalidity of isolated and separated efforts for Christian mission in the world.

While the emergence of world Christian bodies such as the International Missionary Council and later the World Council of Churches was a source of inspiration and enthusiasm for these churchmen of Asia, they also saw that cooperation at the world level should imply for them closer fellowship within their own region. In isolation from one another and from the churches of many backgrounds around the world, it was not always possible for them to have a proper perspective about the situation and problems which their own churches faced. One may repeat the words of Dr. John R. Mott, written in another context: "How greatly Christian leaders need to be drawn out of the meshes of everyday . . . routine . . . and other activities into fellowship with fresh and productive minds of other communions and nationalities. . . ."

Going even more deeply than closer fellowship and creating more frequent opportunities for consultation and contact at the regional or international levels, these churchmen also came to see the need for the churches of different traditions and missionary connections in each land to join together in a unified life for a united witness, even in the face of continued separation of church life and traditions in the West—from where their missionaries came. Dissatisfaction with the fragmentation of Christian life and mission in countries of Asia, and the conviction that the Church of Christ must be one led them to take steps to manifest unity among the separated churches. The case of the inauguration of the Church of South India bringing churches of differing traditions into one organic unity may be cited as the foremost example arising within the Asian region.

Inspiration gained through world Christian contacts led to the actions for local and regional Christian fellowship and cooperation. Ecumenical encounter in global Christian assemblies should not become an excuse for avoiding implications and challenges for unity and cooperation in a given country or an area of the world. Dr. Norman Goodall rightly pointed out that: "Ecumenical encounter has been easier to achieve internationally than locally. There has been more enthusiasm for going to Amsterdam or Evanston that for crossing the road from the local Baptist church to the local Anglican parish church."

Healthy Universalism Presupposes a Healthy Regionalism

In other words, for the Christian world it simply means that ecumenism begins at home—particularly in a situation where through airplane, radio, and television even the remotest parts of the world have become next-door neighbors to one another. This fact of technological progress forms both a major springboard as well as an obstacle for the development of a healthy regionalism and a healthy universalism. In some ways possibilities of easy communications with the remotest parts of the world can lead us to believe that these would facilitate constant interchange of personal contacts and views between peoples and churches around the world—so much so that the cultivation and nuturing of the roots of ecumenism in the various parts or regions of the world need not require much attention. Then in these regions of the world there are those who are readier to fly off to remotest corners of the earth to discuss ecumenism or to join in fellowship with Christians of other confessions and lands rather than remain at home and face up to the discipline and challenge of practicing local ecumenism. Students are eager to secure ecumenical scholarships in distant lands even if these scholarships are not immediately relevant to the needs of their own churches.

What then is healthy regionalism in the Christian world? When the East Asia Christian Conference was formed in Indonesia in 1957 and when a plan was drawn up to form the East Asia Christian Conference (EACC) as an organ of continuing fellowship and cooperation among the churches and Christian councils in East Asia, there were some who asked if the conference was going to be a Christian version of the conference of Afro-Asian nations who gathered earlier at Bandung in Indonesia to assert their corporate role in assessing and shaping the affairs and course of the world of nations. Surely it was unthinkable in the Christian world that a conference should be called to form a fellowship of "colored" Christians in Asia over against the other Christians in the West. The spontaneous inclusion of the churches of Australia and New Zealand in the East Asia Christian Conference from the very beginning of its inception and planning provided ample proof that the consideration in determining the limits of such a regional Christian organ, was, humanly speaking, geography and not race. The *raison d'être* of regionalism in the church universal cannot be politics, culture, economics, or anything of the sort. It must ever be conceived and expressed in relation to *the common evangelistic task*. It was not an accident that led the 1957 East Asia Christian Conference to select as its theme "The Common Evangelistic Task of the Churches in East Asia." There can be no denying of the historical facts associated with the development of the churches in Asia. Asian churches are often attacked by those who see them as appendages of the West and as developments out of the colonial connections. While explaining the character of the Church universal in which all those called by Christ from the nations around the world are found, the Christians in Asia must also interpret the gospel to their fellow countrymen and peoples in their area in terms which they can understand in their own national, cultural, and historical setting. The nationalist with an eye on his own country's history cannot altogether believe that the Cross which was brought by a Western missionary into his country has nothing to do with the colonial flag which arrived around the same time in the wake of European traders. There is no wonder that Asian churchmen all along in ecumenical conferences have emphasized the necessity of their churches being rooted in the soil of Asia as well as in the word of God. The need, then, is to discriminate between the false and the true in the emerging regionalism and "ecumenicity" of our times. True regionalism and true ecumenicity do go together and in history we must contend with the tension between regionalism and "ecumenicity" because of the tendency on the part of both to become false. This, however, needs to be seen as part of the tragedy of human existence and calls for vigilance at all times.

The Strategic Missionary Approach to a Region

Still other pressing questions for Christian mission in Asia call for the creation of opportunities for the churches in the area to come together and examine them without having to think of drawing up statements and programs of action applicable to and valid for churches around the whole wide world. This is not to suggest that Asian questions must be looked at only by

Asians and that the program emerging out of such common consultations be carried out only by them. As it was said at the inaugural assembly of the East Asia Christian Conference, Asian churches and churches in other parts of the world have "both the right and the duty to call upon" one another singly and collectively and also "the ecumenical movement as a whole to pursue a grand strategy of" Christian witness and service. The basic concern is to help the churches around the world to develop a comprehensive Christian strategy for each continent or region of the *oikumene*. This is all the more necessary when we remember that "the natural tendency of world organization is to regard human problems in the mass. It is necessary to deal with human needs (and Christian mission) in terms of local and regional concreteness. This can . . . be done by churches in the same area working together."

In East Asia such a regional agency must seek to examine the theology of mission in the midst of resurgent non-Christian religious systems there. There is a related problem in that the highly analytical and competent statements on the Christian responsibility toward economically and industrially underdeveloped societies may become rather inconsequential when one does not take into account the stranglehold the traditional religious systems have on peoples in these regions of Asian lands. In saying this, one has no desire to minimize the significance of the work and thought that has been produced at the world level. But these statements and studies must find rootage and application in the various areas of the world. Otherwise the prophetic statements on international affairs proclaimed in global terms will be only incomprehensible abstractions. There needs to be the crystallization of Christian vision by those intimately bound up with societies and the history of peoples within specific regions. Here we are concerned not merely with the limitation of area and scope of human situations to which the Christian word is addressed but also with the content and the manner of the word that is addressed. A word spoken at the regional level may be more important than that at the world level.

Issues examined in the light of regional experiences begin to take on new depth and concreteness even when these are the same faced by churches around the world. For example, the renewal of the witness of "the laity" takes on new significance when it is viewed with special reference to congregational life in East Asia where the traditional idea of the religious order or the priesthood often has nothing to do with the imported pattern of a paid ministry of the church. If there is ever a reason for a dilemma between priorities for a global Christian structure and organs for regional action it must always have to do with the search for a meaningful Christian strategy for each continent of the world. In a global structure all cooperating churches and church bodies come together to look at Christian questions in their global framework. Participation in such global conversations itself can unconsciously lead to the drawing of a veil over the eyes of the church bodies (for example, missionary agencies and the confessional world bodies), which in their various ways continue to work separately and alongside one another in different areas and continents of the world. While our unity in Christ is affirmed, our diversity as churches is perpetuated, as churches as well as missionary agencies, including those which acknowledge their membership in or association with the World Council of Churches, continue to project into various parts of the world their several enterprises in the field of education, literature, youth work, and mutual assistance. Consultation and cooperation in a world Christian body, we find, are not necessarily guarantees for the manifestation of unity and coordination at the level of specific regions and continents. Even the very divisions and departments of the World Council of Churches are not exempt from such multiple and simultaneous projections of program and initiatives into the same area. A global structure, under the circumstances and in face of the realities of church history, must provide for and stimulate regional action, enabling the agencies to become those where thinking and planning in a strategic way are done for the missionary approach to their own continents.

Dangers in a Global Structure and Widening Ecumenical Participation Through Regionalization

In a Christian organization with only global structure "the younger churches" will remain almost permanently weaker partners. Dr. Visser 't Hooft rightly pointed out:

The ecumenical conferences of 1937 were too deeply dominated by the crises created by totalitarianism in Europe to give adequate attention to Asian questions. At Madras the central question discussed was one of decisive importance for the Asian churches, the question of the relation of the Christian revelation to the religions, but it was mostly discussed in general theological, rather than in specifically Asian, terms. At the Amsterdam Assembly in 1948 many Asian Christians made significant contributions, but Chandran Devanesan rightly remarked that the East-West conflict as represented in the Dulles-Hromadka debate gave the impression that the East ends at the Bosporus. . . .

Further, in the carrying and execution of the programs developed at the WCC assemblies, there is still room for more participation by churches of the six continents around the world, though we might note that it is increasing. The formation of the EACC has been beneficial in that churches in Asia came to show their realization that the programs for interchurch cooperation and aid are those in which they must participate and that these are not developed by churches in one part of the world simply for the benefit of those in another part. Through such regional organs of cooperation, the churches which usually belong to the "receiving group" came to take actions for sharing experiences, personnel, and even the meager material resources they could muster with others beyond their national and regional frontiers.

Another way in which regionalization has furthered wider fellowship and participation in Christian cooperation is that some of the churches in countries with administrations not so friendly to the governments of the West find it simpler to maintain fellowship with churches in similar historical situations within the same region.

There is yet another area where regionalization could enable wider fellowship. This is related to tension between schools of theology. As Christians of Asia are placed in the midst of overwhelmingly large numbers of those who are adherents of other religions, they stand as question marks among their fellowmen. Why do others continue in their age-old religious behavior and why have these Christians discarded the religious heritage of their countries? Such Christians are compelled to seek to be ready to give an answer to every man who asks them for the reasons for the hope that is theirs. Evangelism is what they must live with. The tensions between "modernism" and "fundamentalism," so called, are largely irrelevant to Christians in Asia. In certain situations it has been noticed that churches which fear contamination with imported "modernism" in global Christian organizations are not too ready to accept the accusation that their fellow Asian Christians are not evangelical. This is not to suggest that "regionalism" is the answer to the tensions that exist between schools of theology. One can only rejoice that, here and there, signs of the Church's response to the moving of the Holy Spirit can be more readily nurtured in concrete missionary situations.

Still other views have been expressed in relation to localizing or regionalizing cooperative Christian efforts while keeping always, of course, the abiding need of churches to be aware of, and experience the fellowship in, the church universal. As ecumenical structure becomes more complex, delimitation and specific application of plans and program for cooperation and unity become all the more necessary and desirable. In another context, the Christo Samaj of India prepared a statement for Dr. J. H. Oldam in 1921 and its words might well apply to our present consideration. The statement warned that "the . . . centralization of authority and the much more complicated and heavy machinery that [is envisaged] will be the culmination and triumph of a foreign system that will clothe young David not only in the armour of King Saul, but still worse, in that of the Philistine Goliath. . . ." The statement went on to emphasize the importance of making room for simpler and spontaneous organizations natural to the soil of the countries around the world.

But such advocacy should not mean welcoming the prospect for the falling away of the universal *koinonia* into unrelated regional fragments. True interdependence must rule out both the assertion of, and the withdrawal into, independence. As Bishop Newbigin said at the East Asia Christian Conference at Kuala Lampur:

There is a false dependence which is the mark of infantility, of arrested development. But there is a true dependence which is one of the marks of health. "We are members one of another." In the mature and healthy body each part is dependent on the whole. Each part has something to contribute, but also much to receive. Once the basic responsibility to God is established, there is then a whole multitude of ways in which mutual interdependence will express itself. . . . Partnership means not simply a relation of mutual helpfulness between two partners but an actual growth into interdependence. . . .

And that is true of the worldwide fellowship of the church.

We are being granted to join in setting up the tabernacle of the Lord here on earth. In the words of Isaiah 54:2, the dual command is to lengthen the ropes and to strengthen the stakes. For the wide spreading of the tabernacle to the uttermost parts of the earth the command also reminds us to drive the stakes deeper in each place. True regionalism must be understood only in relation with obedience to this dual command.

KOINONIA *THROUGH THE IRON CURTAIN*

Elisabeth Adler

Elisabeth Adler is a highly regarded leader in student Christian circles from East Germany. Her present position as Associate General Secretary of the World's Student Christian Federation in Geneva gives her the task—as agonizing as it is rewarding—of preventing Christians from building walls around themselves.

GOD, I thank Thee that I am not like men in the West, exploiters, capitalists, warmongers, or even like those who call themselves Christians and do nothing against the evil of capitalism. I have no private property and I am for peace."

"God, I thank Thee that I am not like men in the East, revolutionaries, communists, oppressors, or even like those who call themselves Christians and do nothing against the evil of communism. I take all that I possess from Thy hands and I am for freedom."

Sometimes I wonder if Jesus would not tell the parable this way today, to the pious in the East and in the West who "trust in themselves that they are righteous and despise others." Of course we Christians in East or West know that the prayer of the Pharisee was not acceptable to God and we would not lay bare before God our self-righteousness. However, we betray ourselves by putting the same Pharisaical attitude into a prayer which seems more similar to the prayer of the publican.

The Eastern Christian may pray:

"God be merciful to Thy Church which does not fight against capitalism, imperialism, and colonialism as it should."

The Western Christian may pray:

"God be merciful to Thy Church which does not resist the communist revolutions as it should."

Or even more likely, we may hide our self-righteousness in intercessory prayer for one another:

"God, open the eyes of Christians in the West to the unholy bond between Christianity and capitalism"; and "God, open the eyes of Christians in the East to the dangers of Christian-Marxist syncretism."

Or another variation:

"Lord, be with the Christians who live in so-called Christian countries amid all the temptations which privilege and official recognition present to them"; and "Lord, be with the Christians who are oppressed by communism, in all their trials and persecutions."

And now it sounds all right. Here we have formulations that shock no one, that are familiar to us, in the East, or in the West. We are pleased with ourselves in a more sophisticated way than was the Pharisee in the parable. After all, we are praying for our neighbors, for our neighbors whom we pity—or should I say for our enemies whom we fear? No, we should avoid calling them enemies: the Christian in the other half of the world is still our neighbor, our fellow Christian, our brother in spite of the capitalist or communist system in which he unfortunately has to live. We are pleased with ourselves because we are generous enough still to call him our brother even though this is unpopular among the people around us. And we are pleased with ourselves because our intercession for our brother on the other side seems to prove our readiness to maintain our fellowship in spite of the despised system in which he lives and which has without doubt an influence upon him.

But honestly—is there a basic difference between the first prayers and these that follow? Is this kind of prayer for one another a sign of existing *"koinonia* through the Iron Curtain"? We should not be took quick to take comfort by reminding ourselves that everything that we do, including our prayer, is imperfect and selfish, and that nothing we do is fit either to establish or to reflect the *koinonia* that we believe is given by God. On the other hand, I do not want to suggest that we have only to pray better and to improve here and there, and then we shall have the *koinonia* we ought to have as fellow Christians. I simply want to show how difficult *"koinonia* through the Iron Curtain"* is and that even our prayers, which we think of as independent of political, social, and ideological realities such as the so-called "Iron Curtain," are prejudiced by our differences and reveal lack of fellowship, isolation from one another, differences in language, outlook, hope, and fear.

We are accustomed in our ecumenical discussions to thinking of theological differences as obstacles to *koinonia,* and put the so-called nontheological factors only in a footnote. I believe, however, that the nontheological factors are much more decisive than is generally admitted, and that the Iron Curtain is one of them.

When we try now to look at the possibilities for *"koinonia* through the Iron Curtain,"* we shall do so from an empirical point of view and not from the theologically defendable, but abstract, thesis: "God creates *koinonia* in spite of. . . ." After all, *koinonia* which is not real—and here I mean discernible, visible, convincing to the sharp and critical eyes of the world— does not make any difference, does not change, does not give hope to our troubled and divided world, is no hint of the reconciling power of God in this world. When speaking about the possibility of East-West relations among Christians, I shall also have to show the obstacles to it. Among the obstacles I do not see in the first place (and I am sorry to disappoint the reader who may have hoped for sentimental and sensational stories about secret crossing of borders and climbing of walls for the sake of Christian fellowship!) is the so-called Iron Curtain. Though it is a border which cannot always be crossed at will, or the wall in Berlin, though it does indeed prevent congregations from worshiping together, the real estrangement is that which has taken place between Christians on both sides, partly because of the different development of society here and there and partly as a result of the cold war, which emotionalizes and exaggerates those differences.

The occasions to meet and to exchange thoughts are indeed limited, but during the last few years the desire to come together, and with it the necessary imagination and opportunities, have increased. I shall mention only two illustrations:

1. The Christian Peace Conference, with its International Secretariat in Prague, has brought together a large number of Christians from East and West since it started its work in 1958. There were as many as three hundred from each side at its assembly in 1961.

2. The Assembly of the WCC welcomed into its membership, as everyone knows, at its meeting in New Delhi several churches from Eastern Europe, among them the Russian Orthodox Church. Several other churches from "behind" the Curtain have since applied for membership. (We should not say "behind," because this either implies that the World Council is Geneva or the fellowship which the churches have through membership in the World Council exists only "before" the Iron Curtain. But more about this later.)

Very obviously the occasions for meeting one another have increased, but what happens when we meet?

I have been in many ecumenical meetings in which Christians from both sides took part. Some were held in the East, some in the West (which makes quite a difference) ; some were attended by equal numbers from both sides, some mainly by Westerners with a few guests from "over there," and some mainly by Easterners with a few visitors from "outside" (which again makes quite a difference). But in general—I have found one overall attitude in the encounter between East and West: a burning desire on the part of the Christian from the East to make himself understood, to overcome the prejudices and to win the confidence of his Western fellow Christian with his outlook of indulgence, politeness, and pity. He, the Westerner, does not take too much trouble to make his point of view understood, supposing that his assumptions are the only possible and reasonable ones for all Christians, and that they are also held secretly by the Eastern Christian who, unfortunately, feels compelled to present the propaganda point of view.

And indeed this supposition is not always wrong. The centuries-old mixture of Western and Christian thought, which most Western Christians do not even recognize in themselves, has survived in a good many Christians who now live in societies which are changing in accordance with Marxist principles. When Western Christians meet this type of Eastern Christian, who lives in a kind of inner emigration, encounter easily becomes possible: the Iron Curtain separates them only geographically. But this is not what I would call true encounter between East and West or *koinonia* through the Iron Curtain. I would see this rather as the natural agreement and understanding between politically like-minded people who happen to be at the same time Christians.

There exists also a comparable type of Westerner who, by the very fact of his strong disagreement with certain aspects of Western life and politics, is sympathetic toward the East, and when he shares his criticism of the West with the Christians from the East he believes he is better understood by them than by many of his fellow Christians in the West. Again this is a kind of inner emigration on the part of the Westerner, and the understanding is merely agreement between politically like-minded people.

The two "types" described—and there are certainly within these types many different "shades"—have something in common: they give a one-sided, untypical interpretation of their

own situation and thus more easily gain sympathy and confidence among people from the other side. But there is, I believe,
one important difference. Openness toward the East is extremely rare among Western Christians these days: sympathy
with the East is almost the unforgivable sin against the Holy
Spirit! The marriage between Christianity and Western liberal
democracy is taken for granted by the majority of Christians
in the West, whereas Christians in communist countries—even
the Chinese who are looked upon by the West as having fully
identified themselves with the cause of communism—would always maintain that Christian faith and Marxist ideology can
never go together (though of course many would support the
social changes in their countries). To most Christians, as well
as to the majority of all people in East and West, it is evident
that Christianity and the West belong together and that Christians in the East are strangers in their environment. The
Church would do well to remember that Christians are *nowhere
anything but pilgrims and strangers.*

No one from the West can hope to enter into dialogue with
Christians from the East as long as he is convinced that the
Western system is the only one which is reasonable, human,
blessed by God, and acceptable for Christians. Therefore I believe that the Western sympathizer, whom I described above,
has some chance for real encounter with a Christian from the
East, even if at first they agree mainly on their criticisms of
the West. They will then go on to discuss the East. The Eastern
Christian will share his problems more easily with someone who
does not have a closed mind and has not, like so many Western
Christians, prejudged the situation in the East before he has
ever known it from his own experience or met anyone from there
(except refugees). This open-minded Western Christian may
have illusions about the East, but he has one great advantage:
he is not afraid to meet his fellow Christians from the East
where they are. (Some less open-minded Westerners, even
though they travel today to see the East, will have difficulty in

meeting the people where they really are, because they are looking for proofs of their own preconceived ideas.)

Here I would like to say a word about the important bearing of the place and circumstances of meeting upon the possibility of real fellowship. Everyone will agree that in order
to understand a person one must meet him in his own environment, but in the case of the encounter between Christians from
East and West most people seem to forget this. It is assumed
that the "Christian" climate in the West is more favorable
for the growth of *koinonia,* or Western Christians believe that
the Christians from the East will feel more at ease in the "free
West," will be able to say what he really thinks and to open his
heart. In fact the opposite is true. As a visitor in the West, he
may give the impression of someone who does not dare to speak
(in fact, he often just does not understand the structures, procedures, and terms of reference of the West and prefers first
to listen), or of someone who is an instrument of his government
(in fact he almost never is; he just uses his own terms of
reference and tries to correct misunderstandings about the
Eastern situation). The Western visitor will find Easterners
more "normal" at home; he will discover that they are not
caught up in the ideological struggle every minute of the day.
He may hear one of his Eastern friends give a lecture in his
congregation on the task of the laity (surprisingly enough he
seems to have followed the ecumenical discussion on this question!), and that may be the same man who lectured on peace during his visit to the West (a clear sign of his dependence upon his
government so the Westerner had thought at the time; now
he begins to see why the question of peace is so important for
his friend). Afterwards they may talk about the spiritual and
moral indifference of young people; that neither the Church
nor the state can awaken their sense of responsibility. And
gradually the Western visitor will discover the similarities in the
societies of East and West which on the surface seem so entirely
different. He may also discover why Christians from the East
are longing for contacts and exchange of opinion; because it

is more obvious in the East than in the West that the Church has to discover new ways which have not yet been tried, has to renew itself completely in order to reflect Christ's love to all men and to bring the good news to those who are completely alienated from its traditional life. The "end of the Constantinian era" is more obvious in the East than in the West, and the necessity to respond to the new situation is more clearly seen. In this new task the Church in the East needs the help, the solidarity, and the criticism of Christian brethren everywhere— who in turn will be helped in their own situation through this critical assistance. There is, of course, also the necessity for Eastern Christians to see the life of the Church in the West for they also have abstract conceptions and prejudices. Eastern visitors to the West have often been surprised to find Christians there deeply involved in the struggle against race prejudice and injustice in their society and in the search for new theological insights and new forms of communicating the gospel in a secularized world. They also were struck by the similarities of the two situations and learned to see the task of the Christians in the West together with their own as being part of the same and common responsibility Christians have everywhere in the world. Meeting in conferences will not be sufficient to provide an understanding of the interdependence of our churches and to enable us to see the task ahead as one service to the world, to be performed by Christians in East and West together, even though in different forms. The best opportunity for "*koinonia* through the Iron Curtain" does not open up when we seek fellowship for the sake of fellowship, but when we are concerned together about our common task.

At this point I have to go back to the question of obstacles to the Christian fellowship across the ideological border. What I have said could be misinterpreted to mean: if only Western Christians would try to be less critical of communism and more critical of their own societies, *koinonia* through the Iron Curtain would become possible. This is not what I intended. I have described wrong attitudes, prejudice, ignorance, and lack of interest in the situation of brethren on the other side in order to show that basic to these attitudes is unbelief in God's power to act in this world through unworthy instruments. We tend to doubt the sincerity of the faith of Christians from the other side and to think that God is on our side. And this self-righteousness and mistrust, or at least doubt, about our fellow Christians is the greatest hindrance to fellowship. I think I am not wrong in saying that most Christians from the West are only convinced of the sincerity of the Christian faith of those Easterners who have expressed strong criticism of the theory and practice of communism and their preference for Western democracy and a liberal economy. The Eastern Christian may not have the same basic doubts, but he tends to think of Western Christianity as rooted merely in tradition and not in faith in the living God. Who are we to judge the faith of our neighbor? Who are we to tell God how and by whom he will build His kingdom? As soon as we accept one another as members of the people of God, though weak and not through our own merits but because we have been called, there is the possibility for *koinonia*. And we are able to accept one another if we place more importance on God's action in the world than on our mutual acceptability.

I do not mean to say that all difficulties in dealing with one another disappear immediately when together we pay attention to God and what he wishes us, his people, to do. But mere politeness to one another (which still prevails in ecumenical meetings) becomes impossible. We shall disagree, but we shall begin to listen to one another. We shall still find one another one-sided, but we shall also discover our own one-sidedness.

In a recent meeting of the Prague Christian Peace Conference, an extensive discussion about our respective one-sidedness took place in the theological commission. Here Christians from East and West after they had with good reason spent some time reproaching one another for one-sidedness, discovered that there is neither an Eastern nor a Western gospel, and therefore neither an Eastern nor a Western theology. They discovered that it is possible in the light of the gospel to take our mutual one-sidedness with good humor, and that such an encounter enables us to take one another seriously as one-sided people, because God's one-sidedness, which is of a different kind, transforms all our narrowness and one-sidedness. God is one-sided in His "Yes" to the world, in His love to all men, in His plan to save and to reconcile the world in Christ, and when we look at his one-sidedness we shall be liberated from our own one-sidedness and conformism. It was felt that such a gathering of Christians from the East and West as the Prague meeting will only truly perform its task if it takes God's one-sidedness as a starting point; it will then be able to say something which does not conform to either East or West, something which is not said either without or against the brother on the other side. As Professor Hromadka has often repeated, this does not imply that all differences of opinion are artificially covered up with brotherly sentimentality and formal Christian piety. Our concern should be to see ourselves, in frank, and perhaps difficult, discussions, in the mirror of the other side, so to speak. We should try not to put aside as distorted the picture which our Christian brother has of us, but to accept it with humility. Through this very often unpleasant picture, we may learn to see how deeply we are caught up in our prejudices and how much we resist God's liberating power in Jesus Christ.

This, I believe, is *koinonia* in action: fully accepted interdependence. This is not an easy way, but one which has promise. It is perhaps easier to leave aside differences of opinion, and we often try to go this way. I remember meetings where there was great anxiety to avoid touching upon points where disagreement was certain. To be concrete: how many Christians in the West hope that the Russian Orthodox representatives will take part in the ecumenical dialogue in the World Council of Churches only as "churchmen," and leave aside their political views! But the world in which the Ecumenical Movement lives and works is not a different one from the world of politics! And we do not seek fellowship in order to have nice, friendly meetings among ourselves, but in order to perform our common task in the world, to witness to God's reconciling love in this world.

I remember one Russian Orthodox representative saying at an ecumenical meeting: "For us Christians the Iron Curtain does not exist"; and another, "We can bring the message of reconciliation to the world because we are reconciled people." Of course the Iron Curtain exists also for us—but its existence is relative, and its consequences—hatred, misunderstanding, and prejudice—can be overcome in our common knowledge of the ultimate truth of God's reconciling purposes for the world.

If, then, the ground of *koinonia* is not the goodwill of man but the act of God, *koinonia* through the Iron Curtain is not only possible but is a fact, has happened before we become aware of it. We then have only to try not to obscure it, but to work out its practical implications and to live accordingly.

This is not a matter only for ecumenical experts who take part in important meetings, but a task for the whole Church in East and West.

The Church as a whole must take the challenge of Marxism seriously. Marxist materialism is a strong reminder of the social dimension of life and of the fact that human existence is conditioned by history, to a Church which has spiritualized the gospel, overemphasized the value of the individual to the neglect of society.

The Church as a whole must give evidence of deep repentance. For Marxists the Church has lost its credibility because Christian peoples have started innumerable wars throughout the centuries, have subjected peoples in Africa and Asia through colonialism, and have not abolished the conditions in which "man is a humiliated, enslaved, abandoned, and contemptible creature" (K. Marx). This repentance should include not only the admission of the failures of past generations but also of our own and a rectifying of our attitudes and actions today.

The Church as a whole must liberate itself from all false alliances. Marxists think of Christianity as a "class religion" and a weapon in the cold war, an ally of the anti-communist front. The Church indeed has often sought alliance with the state and conformed to its ideology, and this is still a danger in East and West. Unless we liberate ourselves from it, we deny the freedom of the children of God.

The Church as a whole must accept the historical situation in which it lives as a commitment from its Lord. It has to proclaim the gospel in service and love in the society in which it is placed, but it must understand its service in each particular situation as part of the whole service of the whole Church in the world.

The Church as a whole must give an example of community and fellowship to the divided and unreconciled world. Christians in East and West should not be afraid that people around them may think of them as fellow travelers because they maintain close relationship with Christians of the other side, but rather trust that their fellowship will contribute better understanding between the two sides.

The Church as a whole must be together the expectant community awaiting the coming of the kingdom of God. All members of the Body of Christ have a concern for one another, sharing suffering and joy, weakness and strength, accepting responsibility together, living in full solidarity, and performing one service in the world, and all are bound together in constant intercession for one another.

We then can witness joyfully to *"koinonia* through the Iron Curtain" as God's act among us, knowing that just as we are involved in the sin of the world, so we suffer together with the world its consequences such as mistrust, hate, alienation, and suspicion. But we know also that we do not have to carry the burden of our sin on our own shoulders because Christ has taken the sin of the world upon himself. Ultimately it is Christ who perforates the Iron Curtain—and this is why we can go into the future with confidence and hope.

THE GREAT DEBATE
ABOUT EMERGING CONCILIARISM

COUNCILS, COUNCILS EVERYWHERE . . .

Ralph Hyslop

> *Ralph Hyslop* is Professor of Ecumenics at Union Theological
> Seminary in New York, and was formerly at Pacific School of
> Religion in Berkeley, California. He worked in the Geneva
> headquarters of the WCC preparing for the Evanston Assem-
> bly and served on the Assembly staff in Evanston. He has
> been responsible for the Program for Advanced Religious
> Studies at Union.

AN unsought tribute to the effective publicizing of the word
"ecumenical" by the World Council of Churches is to be
observed in the fact that Roman Catholic authors are now finding it necessary to explain to the world the special sense in
which the term, Ecumenical Council, is to be understood. Hans
Kung, in his excellent study *The Council, Reform, and Reunion*
(Sheed & Ward, 1961), refers to an address by John XXIII to
the diocesan presidents of Italian Catholic Action. Here, the
Pope refers to "The Ecumenical Council" in terms which reflect
unmistakably his conviction that it must engage in the task of
reform of the Church. Professor Kung, who heartily agrees with
this, must nevertheless point out that false hopes have been
raised among non-Roman Catholics by the very use of the
words "Ecumenical" and "Council" in conjunction. "In Eng-
lish, 'Council' has both the narrower sense of a council of the

Church in its traditional meaning and the wider one of a parliament or assembly, *as in the World Council of Churches* (Italics
mine). 'Ecumenical,' when used in connection with the latter,
means interdenominational; whereas in its ancient traditional
sense in Catholic canon law it means the assembly of all the
Catholic bishops in so far as they are not prevented by external
circumstances from attending."

We might justly remark to the author that, while making a
necessary distinction from his own point of view, he has compounded the problem of definition and understanding in three
ways. First, he has failed to point out that the World Council
of Churches is not a "parliament or assembly" but an organization with many divisions and departments, staff and worldwide
operations. We would be unwise and inaccurate to compare it
to the Roman Curia. Second, this World Council of Churches
does convene representative meetings and it calls them assemblies. It was the meeting of the Third Assembly of the World
Council of Churches at New Delhi, November 19–December 5,
1961, which is perhaps most likely to be confused with the Second Vatican Council. Third, Dr. Kung uses without question
the word "Catholic" to describe the Church which must be given
its full title if we are to avoid really serious confusion. He means
the Roman Catholic Church and he refers to Bishops of that
Church only, when he speaks of "the assembly of all the Catholic bisops." He is surely aware that many other Bishops consider themselves correctly described as "Catholic bishops" and
their Churches as "Catholic Churches."

Has Dr. Kung then failed utterly to distinguish between the
"ecumenical" of the World Council of Churches and the "ecumenical" of Pope John's Ecumenical Council: Vatican II? No,
he has given us a very helpful push toward making some distinctions of our own and facing squarely the meaning of *our* Council
and its assemblies. He has surely represented correctly the view
which the Roman Catholic Church holds regarding itself and
the nature of its councils. And we may hope that he has rightly
discovered in the intentions of the Pope that dedication to the

reform of the Church "in head and members" which was so significant in the conciliar movement of the fourteenth and fifteenth centuries.

It appears, however, that we need to understand a far wider range of meaning in the words "ecumenical" and "council" than Dr. Kung has suggested. Our thought must extend not only over the contemporary scene but back into history as well. It must comprehend not simply a Roman Catholic and a Protestant view of councils but, and perhaps most important of all, an Orthodox understanding. And we cannot look only at councils convened on a worldwide basis but at regional, national, state, and local Councils. What does this perplexing array of councils mean?

First and most obviously, it means that the Church of Christ is divided. This is tragic irony, for both at the beginning and now, these councils have meant to display the Church's unity and not her division. We can surely understand that our Roman Catholic brethren wish to be called simply Catholics and to regard their Council as that of the one Church. For we too are fond of affirming the unity of the Church while testifying silently to its divisions by admitting into membership in the World Council of Churches 198 different churches. The Orthodox, no less than the Roman Catholic, affirms his identity with the One, Holy, Catholic, and Apostolic Church and points to unswerving allegiance to the undivided Church of the Seven Ecumenical Councils and the first eight centuries. Thus, indeed, the Orthodox churches find their place in fellowship with the World Council of Churches, for its members have at least not committed against the unity of Christ's Church the sin which inheres in the claim of divine authority for the Bishop of Rome and the designation as Catholic only of those Christians who accept him as Vicar of Christ and Supreme Pontiff.

Nor must we forget the "lesser" ancient churches of the East, so often and so unjustly called "monophysite." Regarding themselves as true defenders of the apostolic faith and practice, they can accept neither those Seven Councils regarded as truly Ecumenical by the other Orthodox (for Chalcedon, the Fourth, resulted in their unjust condemnation) nor the claims of Rome. Some of them, too, have found fellowship in the World Council of Churches with its minimal doctrinal requirement as a basis of membership. Finally, there are the many churches which for often directly opposite reasons have remained outside the World Council of Churches. The Unitarian-Universalist Christians find that too much is demanded of them as a statement of faith; the Southern Baptists doubt that fellowship on so vague a basis can be truly and fully Christian. If the Roman Catholic Church can hardly be conceived as applying for membership in the World Council of Churches because the others are not truly churches but only "separated brethren," there are Pentecostals who still find membership in it difficult because these *are* churches and, therefore, impervious to the Holy Spirit. All these nonmembers of the World Council of Churches have their own forms of councils. The Ancient Mariner's cry, "Water, water everywhere, Nor any drop to drink," might, without injustice, be paraphrased, "Councils, councils, everywhere, But none to make us one."

There can be no doubt that the grave problems of disagreement on matters of doctrine and practice, which necessitated the convening of the councils of the Church of the early centuries, differ in one most significant respect from all the problems faced by later councils. However serious the differences or arbitrary the means of their solutions, the early councils labored under the conviction of an essential and *existing* unity of the Church of Christ. The first part of this conviction has never been lost; history has made the second untenable. It matters not whether the council was convened under the authority of the Apostles, as at Jerusalem, the Emperor, as at Nicaea, or the joint authority of Emperor and Pope, as at Chalcedon—the assumption was that there could be and actually was but one Church throughout the world. A council, properly convoked and assembled, could therefore speak with that authority granted to the Son by the Father and exercised effectively by the Apostles and their successors with the guidance of the Holy Spirit. Such Councils could and did rule not only that certain interpretations of the faith were opposed to apostolic teaching but also that, if held to after being denounced as errant, they must cost their holders exclusion from the Church. In the process of preservation of the faith, division of the visible Church took place.

The divisive character of even the most universally accepted councils is sadly illustrated by Chalcedon and its aftermath. Persecution of dissenters was fierce. Not only were persons destroyed but also libraries containing the treatises in which the dissenters sought to present fully their views and defend their orthodoxy. To this day it is extremely difficult to obtain any other than an official Chalcedonian presentation of the doctrines that Council condemned. It is as though the entire record of the case of the defense in a murder trial should be given to historical record by the prosecution.

The expulsion, 1,500 years ago, of the Syrio-Aramic Church from imperial Christendom left intact the unity of East and West, affirmed in the councils succeeding that of Chalcedon. Indeed, so central to Orthodoxy is the recognition of the first seven councils as ecumenical that the churches of this family often refer to themselves as "the Church of the Seven Councils." All these councils were held in the Eastern portion of the Roman Empire and all dealt to a considerable extent with problems of faith and life arising in that area. In them the faith was authoritatively defined and the Holy Spirit's guidance so unmistakably present that all later councils and all decisions confronting the Orthodox Church have their ecumenical character and practical determination established in relation to them. Although the Great Schism between the Eastern Orthodox and the Roman Church didn't take place until 1054, the seeds of division were deeply sown and visibly developing into full bloom under the pressures of cultural and political as well as theological divergencies.

It is tempting to all non-Roman Christian churches to assign to the dogma of papal sovereignty sole responsibility for this and later divisions of the visible Church. Actually, as careful examination of the Great Schism and of the Protestant Reformation will reveal, the causes of division are multiple and exceedingly complex. But it is true, even after allowances are made for antipapal bias, that the steady enlargement of papal claims and the insistence upon obedience to the Bishop of Rome as to Christ Himself provided the main basis for reform measures which finally issued in division. No period of history and no group of councils illustrates this so vividly as the fourteenth and fifteenth centuries and the councils of Constance and Basel-Ferrara-Florence. The movement of reform known in history as The Conciliar Movement is still seen by Roman Catholic theologians as a menace to the God-given structure of the Church and by non-Roman scholars as a true reform impulse and a precursor of the modern ecumenical movement.

In these sharply opposing views of the Conciliar Movement we may find in essence the principles that divide us still. The Conciliarists saw Christendom tragically rent by division stemming from the very source of its unity: the Church of Christ. When Marsilius of Padua wrote in his treatise, *Defensor Pacis*, that the Pope was guilty of "defacing the beauty of the Church, which is her unity," he seemed almost to be predicting the Papal Schism of 1378. With national groups allied behind rival Popes, men viewing the potential dissolution of the very society in which they lived called for reform of the Church and reunion of the Christian commonwealth, with supreme authority in the Church residing in a General Council truly representative in character. So the Council of Constance, in 1415, claimed to represent the Catholic Church militant and to hold authority directly from Christ. Its edict left no possible doubt of its claim and intention: ". . . all men of every rank and condition including the Pope himself, is [*sic*] bound to obey it in matters concerning the Faith, the abolition of the schism, and reformation of the Church of God in its head and its members."

The accomplishments of Constance were hardly less impressive than its program. The Papal Schism was ended by the deposition of two Popes and the resignation of the third. Concordats with five nations were drawn up and, most important, the decree *Sacrosancta* proclaimed the superiority of Council over Pope and that entitled appropriately *Frequens* called for the regular convocation of councils. It is significant that in contemporary view the crowning achievement of this brilliant assembly was the election of a new Pope, Martin V. He, of course, repudiated the conciliar theory of the decree, *Sacrosancta,* and denied the right of appeal from Pope to Council. He did, however, accede to the other decree and in accordance with its provision for the meeting of a council every five years, issued invitations to a council which, after some delays and changes of location, finally met at Basel under his successor, Eugene IV, in 1431. This strong-willed prelate made known with vigor his rejection of conciliarism and, transferring the Council to Ferrara in 1437, demonstrated the sovereign power of the papacy by negotiating the reunion of the Greek and Latin churches in 1439. The Conciliar party, still in a formal majority according to their reconstruction of Council membership and voting power, employed perhaps their only possible stratagem in seeking the deposition of the Pope and the establishment of one willing to accept the role of constitutional monarch. But Nicholas V could never successfully challenge Eugene IV and the failure of the Conciliar movement was certain.

Yet, as so often in history, failure in one century presages victory in another. It was the Conciliar principle of Church government which the Reformers of the sixteenth century espoused, and it was a free and universal council for which they called. In very familiar words, Martin Luther, writing deferentially to Leo X in 1520, counsels the Holy Father thus: "You are a servant of servants. Do not listen to those who say that none can be Christians without your authority, who make you the lord of heaven, hell, and purgatory. They err who put you above a council and the universal Church." In his *Appeal to the*

German Nobility in the same year, he says: "Therefore when need requires, and the Pope is a cause of offense to Christendom, in those cases whoever can best do so, as a faithful member of the whole body, must do what he can to procure a true free council. This no one can do so well as the temporal authorities, especially since they are fellow-Christians, fellow-priests . . . ."

This is Conciliarism and, though the depth of the offense to faith and the ardor of the reformer were to combine with political causes to make this protest against Papal excesses an occasion of deep schism as well as true evangelical awakening, the purpose in view is the same for Gerson and Luther, Marsilius of Padua and Calvin of Geneva. Even the threats of Constance and the warnings from Wittenberg are strikingly similar. *Sacrosancta*, in 1415, after making it quite clear that the Pope himself was not exempt from its edict, declared "that anyone of any rank and condition, who shall contumaciously refuse to obey the orders, decrees, statutes or instructions, made or to be made by this holy Council, or by any other lawfully assembled general council . . . shall, unless he comes to a right frame of mind, be subjected to fitting penance and punished appropriately: and, if need be, recourse shall be had to the other sanctions of the law. . . ." Luther, in the *Appeal to the Christian Nobility* in 1520 put it with characteristic exuberance: "It must have been the archfiend himself who said, as we read in the canon law, 'Were the pope so perniciously wicked as to be dragging hosts of souls to the devil, yet he could not be deposed.' This is the accursed, devilish foundation on which they build at Rome, and think the whole world may go to the devil rather than they should be opposed in their knavery. If a man were to escape punishment simply because he was above his fellows, then no Christian might punish another, since Christ has commanded that each of us esteem himself the lowest and humblest of all: Matt. xviii:4; Luke ix:48."

Pius II issued the Bull "Execrabilis" in 1460, disposing of the conciliar position in these words, "There has sprung up in our time an execrable abuse, unheard of in earlier ages, namely that some men, imbued with the spirit of rebellion, presume to appeal to a future council from the Roman pontiff, the vicar of Jesus Christ, . . . we condemn appeals of this kind and denounce them as erroneous and detestable. . . ." Leo X, in 1520, answered his opponent, Brother Martin Luther, in words which quite naturally have a more personal tone and a quality of regal exasperation befitting the character of the German monk whose actions inspire the analogy with the wild boars the Prince of the Church is hunting as his lodge at Magliana: "Arise, O Lord, and judge thy cause. A wild boar has invaded thy vineyard . . . he has the temerity to appeal to a future council although our predecessors, Pius II and Julius II, subjected such appeals to the penalties of heresy. Now, therefore, we give Martin sixty days in which to submit, dating from the time of the publication of this bull in his district. Anyone who presumes to infringe our excommunication and anathema will stand under the wrath of Almighty God and of the apostles Peter and Paul."

Reform embodied in actual separation from the Church of Rome proceeded apace as secular princes perceived the opportunity afforded them for defiance of that supreme sovereignty claimed by the Pope but no longer enforceable by the dread decree of interdict. Whole nations were severed from the eternal-temporal realm conceived by Augustine and realized in the high Middle Ages. A Charles V, with all his alleged and actual titles and powers, could not preserve his Catholic Empire from dissolution save by reluctant and disguised assent to inexorable fact: the establishment of evangelical realms with alliances sealed by common religious and political conviction.

But what were these beliefs that bound the German rulers with their peoples, under the inspiration of the work and writings of such men as Luther and his colleagues? The Augsburg Confession gives them noble utterance, and for the other realms the names ring out with all the authority which the restatement of Biblical and Apostolic faith can convey: The Helvetic Confessions, the Heidelberg Catechism, the Westminster Confession, the Thirty-nine Articles, and in the New World, the Cambridge

Platform. Despite their excellence and their inestimable effect in rallying the fighting forces of an often embattled Christian people, they represent in one important sense a tragic defeat for the very movement which gave them birth. For the Protestant Reformation sought precisely what the Conciliarists desired: reformation of the Church in head and members *and* the reunion of Christendom. Luther called for a free and universal council, rejecting Trent because he was convinced it would be neither. Calvin went even further in seeking not only to unite the evangelical movements in all lands but to negotiate true reconciliation with Roman Catholic leaders. No great reformer of the sixteenth century failed to stress the given unity of the Church of Christ and the necessity of visible manifestation of this unity. Most important, despite the rivalries of secular princes and their own too great dependence upon them as a practical necessity, none failed to call these rulers to their duty as "fellow-Christians, fellow-priests" to assist and even initiate the conciliar process which would bring about true reform in the unity which alone can give it final validity.

The Church of Rome proceeded with reform and regained some lost ground. Christians separated from her gave life and power to a faith which was surely apostolic. But the separation continued and widened; Europe was rent by conflict and the faith was deformed by divisions political and ecclesiastical. No one voicing his grief at all this will deny the wonderful power of the living Christ to create anew the congregation which hears His voice and seeks in willing obedience to do His will. Each of the denominations has its glory, its heroes of the faith, its unique gifts. But two essential powers are denied to all of them. They cannot, singly, be in majestic truth the One, Holy, Apostolic Church. They cannot, in their separation from each other, bind the world together: this world which they proclaim to be Christ's. The Roman Catholic and Orthodox doctrine may deny it, but they too are involved with us in this tragic and wholly unintended repudiation of the very nature and the great commission of the Church.

But there *are* councils. There was convened in one twelve-month period, in 1961-1962, a Third Assembly of the World Council of Churches, an Ecumenical Council of the Roman Catholic Church, and numerous national and international assemblies of Churches and councils of Churches. It is possible here to note only the fact of these Councils, their great promise, and their somber reminder of what they cannot be. For no one, viewing the Christian Churches with complete sympathy and rigorous objectivity, can designate one or all of these as *the* free and universal Council of the Church of Jesus Christ. No one even seems to expect that such a council may convene in the forseeable future.

It is my contention that such expectation must be so lively that no practical problems and especially no absorption in present councils, however salutary their effects, will be permitted to diminish it. We will pray for the unity of Christ's Church, we will labor for it, we will manifest it within our present churches and councils, and we will expect such great things from God that it may appear among us in our time.

Let the World Council of Churches and all its members remember that "the ecumenical reformation" is not a fact because of the World Council's existence but a process which may or may not be furthered by the WCC. Hurt as it may, we must daily recall in repentance and prayer that the claimed sovereignty of our denominations is the great denial of Christ's Lordship, a denial which is perpetuated in the World Council of Churches itself. It has become commonplace in our day to insist that the Church must be one if the world is to be called to unity. Let all of us who call upon the name of Christ and seek to be His disciples reiterate that He came that the *world* might be saved. There is no indication that His Church was to concentrate on pulling itself together, hoping then to accomplish that mission of reconciliation of a divided humanity. Without the false pride that declares that we can do what we know only God in Christ can accomplish, let us nevertheless so concentrate our prayers and labors in the fulfillment of our mission that the unity of the

Church will become as truly a work of Christ as is the world's salvation. With no diminishing of the fruitful theological study and promotion of actual unions which has given the past half century a special and glowing character in church history since the Reformation, let us press on even more vigorously in the work of that preaching, teaching, healing, reconciling, which is truly apostolic. And let us do it together and with a sense of urgency at least equivalent to that which marks a world fearful of final catastrophe, yet hopeful for peace and plenty. The impatient critic of the Christian churches ought to be speaking in far gentler terms than we ourselves of that ecclesiastical busy-work which flows from too anxious concern for the Church as it has been. It's like "the little man who wasn't there"; that precious entity was never the Church and it never will be. If it is something that must guard its prerogatives and look with wary eye upon those who would change it, Christ knows it not and the world heeds it not.

The historical lesson of Conciliarism is perfectly stated in the best attested saying of Jesus. On this central point, the four Gospels are clear for the words are spoken by the one who embodied their meaning and enacted their message and gave it, from Calvary, to all who would take upon themselves His ministry: "If any man would come after me, let him deny himself and take up his cross and follow me. For whosoever would save his life will lose it; and whosoever loses his life for my sake and the gospel's will save it." It will never be easy to apply this teaching to the Church itself, yet to whom may it more certainly be applied? For no doctrine of the Church can avoid some form of identification with the one who spoke these words. With no assurance of what the saving of the Church may mean in specific terms, we *can* be assured that it will involve death and resurrection, not a prudent husbanding of rights and resources certain to issue in death and nothing more. Since the Gospel is clearly for the world, we can and must give ourselves at once for Christ and for that world, without counting the cost nor asking any assurance of the final outcome.

DOES THE WORLD COUNCIL HAVE A FUTURE?

Lewis S. Mudge, Jr.

Lewis S. Mudge, after a term on the Geneva secretariat of the Presbyterian World Alliance, is now at Amherst College as Chaplain and Assistant Professor of Religion. In Geneva he was in a key position to study the relations between world confessional groups and the WCC—one of the most delicate items on the ecumenical agenda.

*T*HERE is an obvious, yet dangerous paradox in ecumenical affairs today which needs to be looked at closely. On the one hand, never before has the World Council of Churches had more prestige, forged ahead more effectively on a multitude of fronts, or been more genuinely useful to its member churches. But on the other hand, the movement toward actual unity between churches as such, is, at the moment of writing, virtually stalled.

The first part of this paradox needs no special defense among friends of the ecumenical movement. The latter part need be defended only by pointing to facts. The Ceylon Scheme in its present form is apparently virtually dead. The North India Plan is by no means out of the woods. Conversations between Anglicans and Presbyterians in Great Britain are only now creaking to a new start after the punishing blow dealt them in 1959 by the General Assembly of the Church of Scotland. The best predictions for unity discussions in the United States speak of a long hard road ahead. What is worse, in few of these discussions, with the possible exception of those in Australia, is there much evidence that real breakthroughs have been achieved either in thought or method.

We are in the position of trying again and again to find unity on the basis of formulas that have not proved entirely satisfactory to anyone.

A debate, of course, has gone on for years as to whether the unity we seek should be "organic" or "federal." We have come to see, however, that these possibilities no longer exist as simple alternatives. Organic structures will usually have federal elements, and federal relationships may sometimes grow into organic ones. The real question is the practical one of how our efforts to achieve unity should now be directed, and of how the various elements in this task should be related. Head-on attempts to bring the churches together have met with tremendous frustration. Is this a sign that we must begin to seek churchly unity by frankly conciliar means? Or is the opposite true: that continued failure to bring about unity by direct negotiation will in time undermine our conciliar organizations and distort their purpose no matter how prosperous and powerful they become?

Conciliar forms of ecumenicity are here to stay. This is not to say, of course, that the World Council has already become like the eternal hills, for it is only a youngster of fifteen "summers": on the human scale right in the middle of awkward adolescence. It is surely a mistake to think of the WCC, its structure, its methods of work, or even its existence, as something immutable. Many another organization that once had an air of permanence has vanished from the scene without much trace. Yet it is certainly possible to say that if the World Council ceased to exist, something very much like it would quickly come into being. For this function, this organization, is *needed*, and the need will not go away. Even if the churches unite on a large scale, many of the practical functions of the Council will be needed as much as ever. Conciliar relationships between the churches are bound to exist *alongside* relationships of organic unity for the forseeable future, even if the conciliar structures have to find new and evolving forms.

There is no doubt, moreover, that the WCC as an organization is committed to the goal of the "churchly" unity. The word "churchly" is no longer current, but it still describes in the briefest way what is meant by the New Delhi statement: that the unity sought is that of Christ's Church, not of any Christian organization. Debate about what this means will go on. Enthusiasm for work on the unity question will flag. Despair will creep in where determined energy had been before. But the covenant into which the churches have entered does involve a commitment to seek to overcome the things that separate them, and no one can have any doubt as to where the WCC officially stands. The Council will continue to exist indefinitely, but for it to *substitute* itself for the unity of Christ's Church would be a total departure from its charter, and an abandonment of the vision that has made it great.

The Scaffolding and the Skeleton

The classical treatment of the relationship between councils and churchly unity has been the work of one whose ecumenical eyeteeth were cut on the church union side of the fence. Bishop Lesslie Newbigin, in his books *The Reunion of the Church* (1948, revised edition, 1960) and *The Household of God* (1953) has made it quite clear that in his view councils are an indispensable expression of the churches' determination to make the one Church visible, but not in any sense the *form* which church unity should finally take. Ultimately, the churches themselves must decide what the one great Church is to be, and, in conversations with each other, seek to achieve it. Councils, so long as they last, are always means and never ends. Those who are content with conciliar relationships and who desire to push no further in the matter of unity perhaps do not understand what the Church is. In informal discussion this has been called the "scaffolding" view of the purpose of councils. The scaffolding helps make it possible to build the building, but it is not part of the building. When the time comes that it is no longer needed, it is presumably taken away.

In this situation of ferment, a book has been published which takes quite a different line. President Henry P. Van Dusen, in his study, *One Great Ground of Hope* (1960), is not content to think of councils as mere scaffolding. They are, more nearly, the framework or skeleton of the one Church that is to be. Dr. Van Dusen notes with some nostalgia that councils of churches are no longer dominated by ecumenical prophets who sit loose to the governing structures of their own denominations. On the contrary, councils are now run, on the whole, by men who are also high executives in the churches from which they come. The result has been an inevitable decline in the spirit of adventure, an institutionalization of the councils which stands in marked contrast to the pioneering days. But, if the writer understands correctly, Dr. Van Dusen proposes to make a virtue of this situation by urging the churches to devolve more and more of their administrative functions upon these councils and particularly upon the World Council. He foresees a time in which church executives will make nearly all their important decisions in common with the executives of other churches: when all manner of churchly activities will be conceived, launched, and administered by conciliar instrumentalities. In this way, Dr. Van Dusen suggests, the kind of unity that counts, a "functional" unity, will develop. Local and national councils will then no longer be on the periphery of the life of the churches. They will do most of the things that the administrative hierarchies of the churches now do separately. Something of the development which can be seen in embryonic form in the World Council would then be extended throughout the various levels of conciliar organization from the world level to the local level.

It should be noticed that Dr. Van Dusen's point of view involves, at least potentially, something more than a purely federative concept of unity. For if the churches poured more and more of their functions *as churches* into councils, it follows that councils would take on increasingly churchly form. Dr. Van

Dusen does not suggest that he would ultimately wish to with-
hold any ecclesiastical function or prerogative from conciliar
implementation. The logic of this proposal is certainly that
such functions as confirmation, ordination, and the celebration
of the sacraments might come to be exercised *within* the conciliar
relationship. The result of such a development, even if the
churches retained the specifically churchly powers in principle,
would be that councils would function *as churches*, and thus
effectively become the Church.

There is one glaring fact about Dr. Van Dusen's book, however, that has been surprisingly little noticed. It is that *the question of actual union between churches* is hardly mentioned. It
is as if Dr. Van Dusen had quietly given up hope that union on
any large scale can be a real possibility. It is possible, of course,
that he believes that achievement of churchly unity would follow
readily in the aftermath of the establishment of functional
unity. But if churchly unity is not in view at all, this writer can
think of nothing more ominous for the life of Christendom.
Specifically, if we are no longer concerned about seeking to be
one Church, we have no hope whatever of extricating the true
form of the Church from the administrative structures which
now do so much of the Church's work.

If it were necessary simply to choose between the "scaffolding" and the "skeleton" as images for the relation of councils
to unity, there is no doubt that the "scaffolding" would have the
better claim. But it is no longer possible to rest content with
this alternative. There is real pressure upon us to take a further
step. It is a fact, for example, that a good many of the present
activities of the World Council of Churches are unmistakably
churchly, and meant to be so. Such a claim might be made for
some aspects of the work of Interchurch Aid, and may soon
have to be made for the work of the Division on World Missions
and Evangelism. Moreover, quite a few of the churchly things
the World Council of Churches does have never been done before
by the churches themselves. These functions have not been *ceded*
to the Council from outside. They have been undertaken in

direct obedience to the Gospel in the presence of human need. And now the so-called "churches" are beginning to copy some of these very patterns of organization and action, thus taking elements of "conciliar ecumenicity" into their own churchly systems! A body that can have such a relationship to the churches is more than a mere scaffolding. But it is going too far on the other hand to identify it as the skeletal framework of the one Church. It is something in between, and perhaps is only to be understood in a more theologically fundamental context than that in which these images can help us operate.

The Churches Discover the Church

The new context we need may possibly come into view if we cease thinking of councils and unity negotiations as alternative preoccupations and try to find a theological characterization of the whole reality they represent: the ecumenical *movement*. The word "movement" is not used here in any polemic sense. It is not meant to suggest anything *over against* the institutional or the churchly, but rather to point to a level of theological understanding which includes both. The word is used to refer above all to the fact that God's people move onward in history toward the purpose God has in store for them, and that the ecumenical vision lies at the heart of our understanding of *this* movement in our time. The ecumenical movement is not simply a bundle of large-scale ecclesiastical programs, nor is it a kind of para-ecclesiastical scheme for promoting certain goals which Christians can support as individuals. The ecumenical movement *is* the march of God's people toward the end of history seen in terms of certain particularly pressing needs of this people at the present historical moment: The need for a renewal in mission, the need for a renewal in unity, and so on. On this level of discourse, what goes on in the building of councils and what goes on in unity discussions may turn out to be theologically the same.

It is a constant temptation to say that what the churches are seeking in the ecumenical movement is a new theology, a better ecclesiology, a fresh theory of mission, a new approach to social questions. After all, many of the circumstances in which we now work, considered both in terms of the development of theological scholarship and in terms of the contemporary human condition, seem to point both to the need for such a new outlook and to the possibility of achieving it. Thus the development of biblical theology, combined with new insights into the meaning of the history of dogma, might well indicate that we are on the brink of an understanding of the Gospel which will transcend the partial understandings represented by our denominational and confessional positions.

The ecumenical movement is certainly not seeking to develop any *single* theology or ecclesiology which could be taken to be the normative ecumenical view. Even a superficial reading of the papers coming from the various departments of the Division of Studies of the WCC will show that thinking within the ecumenical movement is incurably pluralistic. This is as true in the realm of sociology and social ethics as it is in the realm of exegesis and the handling of church traditions. When we speak of ecumenical "agreements" we mean something deeper than the conversion of all the participants in a discussion to the same point of view. This needs to be emphasized, for otherwise there is real danger that ecumenical conversations will become exclusively the province of proponents of a particular school of thought. But at the same time, "agreement" in the ecumenical movement does not mean the leveling out of all issues to a lowest common denominator. Such a leveling out would not be agreement, but simply theological anarchy. Yet there *is* a new and distinctive understanding of the Gospel in ecumenical work, an understanding that is consistent with pluralism in every aspect of theological approach and method. How is this possible?

It is possible because the churches have discovered the Church. This, far beyond every achievement in common Biblical interpretation, beyond every device for uniting separated ministries, is the heart of the new thing that the ecumenical movement has brought into being. Churches have become aware that in acting and speaking together they receive a divine gift that is more than the sum total of what they bring to each other: the gift of being *the* Church of Jesus Christ at a given time and place. There is something here that is frankly beyond the power of our present theological equipment to elucidate. One can only say that the gift, the given fact, always goes beyond our logic, always brings into existence what, in purely human terms, cannot exist. It becomes possible to entertain the thought that the divisions between the churches exist *within* the one Church, that theologians from many traditions can think and write as theologians of the one Church, that the churches, met together, can speak as the one Church to the world. This divine gift, a possibility that is received in faith and certainly not by sight, is discernible at every level of the ecumenical movement: in union discussions between churches, in interconfessional conversations, in WCC assemblies, in conferences on social issues.

Our discernment of this divine gift has a further important consequence. When we discover the Church in the midst of the churches, we discover the existence of the Church *in each other*. We are driven to acknowledge that the divine gift, which we supposed momentarily to be something new, has already been given to each of us. We have already been the Church by the grace of God whether or not we fully understood the meaning of what we were, and the same has been true of the other churches we now meet.

This discovery of the Church by the churches can be illustrated at many points in ecumenical life.

One example is the consultation which took place at Cottesloe, near Johannesburg, South Africa, in December, 1960. The matter under discussion was the stand of the churches on the policy of *apartheid*, but the question had been turned into an ecclesiological one by the sharp fissure that had appeared between the Dutch Reformed and the Anglican churches on this issue. Estrangement between these bodies had deepened to such an extent that Anglican representatives had at one point called for the expulsion of the Dutch Reformed from the WCC. Even at the opening of the consultation feelings ran so high that it was by no means certain that either body could regard the other as within the one Church. Yet in the course of the meeting, the sense of the one Church to be discerned within and among the churches unmistakably appeared. For those who signed the statement issued by the conference, there was an awareness that the one Church had spoken in this place in a way that transcended anything that could have been done by the churches separately. Moreover, with representatives of the WCC present, there was a feeling that the Church had spoken in its catholic, or universal dimension. It is not too much to say that this is *the* reality from which one has to begin in any reassessment of the work of councils of churches in relation to actual reunion.

Are Union Negotiations Really Necessary?

But now a pressing question arises. It has been claimed that the churches already can discern the one Church in the midst of them. It had even been said that they can, on occasion, speak and act as the Church of God. Is this not enough? Why, if all this is possible, is it necessary for churches to go through the agonizing business of coming to terms with each other on such matters as the ministry, the sacraments, and the confessions of faith? In comparison with the exciting rediscovery of the givenness of the Church universal, union negotiations are an exasperating, even a grotesque business. They occasionally bring out the worst in those who participate. Seldom do they involve all the Christian bodies in a given area, and even when completed successfully in one place they may not win the approval of churches in other places. Negotiating for actual church union is a painstaking, step-by-step process, a road studded with ruts, a bottomless pit into which the energies of the churches can be poured for years without tangible result.

It may be that some who are close to the secretariat of the World Council of Churches do not realize the extent to which such views prevail, particularly in the Western world. Indeed, insights such as those in the preceding section may appear to strengthen the position of those who believe in the one Church but not in "organic union" between churches. In any event, the case for union has to be made anew every time such negotiations are contemplated. Nothing is more perilous than to assume that the man in the pew understands *why* such negotiations are necessary, much less that he understands this necessity clearly enough to be willing to support the protracted and difficult conversations that nearly always ensue.

It is important, of course, to acknowledge that the churches *can* discover the Church without unifying their ministries and sacraments. If there is pressure to go further than this, that pressure cannot come from outside, but from *within* each particular denomination. The ecumenical movement at large has no theological right to demand that churches make changes in their internal ordering, but the denominations as such may come to see that *what they already believe about themselves,* when seen in the light of the ecumenical situation, demands that they reach out toward their immediate Christian neighbors.

A church should enter a union negotiation when, and only when, it has made up its mind that it must move: not because anyone is forcing such a move from the outside but because the logic of its own tradition, understood in an ecumenical context, makes such movement imperative. A church will often find that its own position suddenly appears to be full of contradictions, and its attitude toward other churches likewise. The process of negotiating for union is surely 90 percent a matter of seeking to resolve these internal contradictions in such a way that the churches in the dialogue can understand and trust each other. It is not more than 10 percent a matter of devising the actual union plan.

There is no ecumenical "theory," imposed from above, that demands "reunion all around." Immediate entry upon union negotiations is not a condition of membership in the WCC, and, indeed, should never be so. But churches themselves discover that they must seek union with other churches if what they have stood for over the centuries is not to be dissolved in ultimate contradiction. The impetus comes, as it were, not from above but from below. Theologically, the internal contradictions that go with disunity appear most sharply where the sacraments *are* celebrated, the Word preached and Christ's ministry carried out: that is to say in the parish, the city, or the region. If we ask the ecumenical movement as a whole for the theological rationale of this or that union negotiation, there can be no universally applicable answer. But if we ask the churches concerned, we will receive a very specific answer: an answer born out of the theological agony of trying to *be* the universal Church in a given place, year in, year out, ecumenical organizations, conferences, and pronouncements notwithstanding.

Does the World Council Have a Future?

Councils of churches are instruments of the churches for giving expression to their common discovery of the Church and for facilitating various steps, including union negotiations, of putting that discovery into practical effect. Does this make them a permanent part of the ecclesiastical scene? Does it make them part of the one Church that is to be?

It is necessary for many practical as well as theological reasons to insist that the WCC is neither *a* church nor *the* Church. To say either of these things would be to defeat the purposes of the Council at once. But, on the other hand, the ecumenical movement has taught us things about the Una Sancta which make it impossible to maintain that the WCC is not churchly at all. At the very least, it participates in churchly reality. The churches already devolve certain "ecclesiastical" functions upon it, and take some of its "conciliar" functions into their own ways of working. Moreover, the Council is not indifferent to the fate of the one Church of Jesus Christ. It exists to promote the strength, effectiveness, and visibility of this one Church.

The WCC is not a static organization. It is not enough to say that it is a kind of bridge thrown between separated churches which will become unnecessary when these churches have come together. Already the Council has taken a multitude of functions which were not envisaged at its inauguration in 1948. It has grown in size and in breadth of membership. It has become the logical channel of ecclesiastical contact between East and West, and one of the important channels between Rome and non-Roman Christendom. It has become a spokesman for its member churches on matters of international politics. It has been the hand and the heart of the churches in world service. It has been the arena for theological movements of potentially great significance. With the growth of unity between the churches as such, the need for such an agency will grow, rather than diminish. If a largely reunited Christendom should wish to be represented at the world level by something other than a "council of churches," it would no doubt still make use of the structures of the World Council as they existed at that time, only giving them a different authority and a different name. But why should even this much change be necessary?

Organic unity is something we seek primarily because the Gospel requires us to break one bread and confess one faith in each place. Where we are dealing with a single, organic unit of society, the unity of the Church must also be organic. But the structures which express the oneness of the Church over wider areas will necessarily differ from those which express it in the local parish. Provided the Church *is* one "in each place," unity does not demand centralization of organization at the national or world levels, but only the possibility of free exchange of ministers and people and the capacity of the various units of the Church to speak and act together when the occasion requires. At the world level particularly, a "council of churches" might well be the inevitable and proper visible form of the Una Sancta. If the time should come that Christendom had to debate what form its world expression should take, the choice would be between a centralized power structure and an essentially conciliar, consultative relationship. Need we ask what the choice of a great part of Christendom would be?

It is not fair to criticize the WCC for not as yet speaking more frankly about such possibilities, for the task of bringing churches into the organization is far from done. It is necessary to hasten slowly. But there is a sense in which we must not let our attention be so centered on the problem of Christian divisions as it exists today that we regard this condition as the only possible background for imaginative reflection. Allowing immediate problems to loom too large may make them harder, not easier to solve. In some ways we make the problem of uniting the churches much too difficult, and at the same time take the theological task of the whole Church much too lightly. Achieving Church unity involves intricate theological tasks, but ultimately it is a matter of willingness to acknowledge that the Church can only be the Church by the grace of God: which is something we can neither bring into being by theological analysis nor bestow upon each other. The real theological task of Christendom, however, is something broader than this, something which *presupposes* our unity and therefore does not have to be preoccupied with ecclesiological argument. It is to get on with understanding the meaning of the Gospel, in terms of man, history, and the created world. It is to face the hermeneutical problem, and the problem of the nature of dogma.

But the WCC and other councils are in a position to offer the churches such an earnest of this future unity that the truly churchly questions can begin to be dealt with at once. These organizations are able not only to create the preconditions for the achievement of unity: they are able to anticipate some of the possibilities which will exist when unity is actually attained. Here lies an essential aspect of their importance. It is indispensable for the churches to begin thinking and acting as the Church, not when all the difficulties between them are solved, but now. Insofar as councils, and the WCC in particular, can make this possible, they are already *of the Church*. They will surely be increasingly considered in this light.

COUNCILS AND THE INNER
PROTESTANT DILEMMA

Walter Leibrecht

Walter Leibrecht, educated in Germany, has taught at the
Harvard Divinity School, and after the Evanston Assembly
was the first Director of the Ecumenical Institute at Evanston.
He is now teaching at the Divinity School of the University of
Chicago.

A_T the New Delhi Assembly of the World Council of
Churches there was widespread awareness that the ecumenical
movement has reached a certain impasse which cannot be overcome merely through new organizational efforts. Unity is more
than organization. There was a new recognition that unity is
basically a dynamic and spiritual reality and that new ways
must be found to reach actual understanding and real communication among Christians and churches of different backgrounds. The polite coexistence of the churches, which we have
achieved through the conciliar associations, is something to be
grateful for. But it can be considered only a step toward deeper
unity. An important statement from the report of the Section
of Unity reads:

> We believe that the unity which is both God's will and His gift
> His Church is being made visible as all in each place who are
> baptized into Jesus Christ and confess Him as Lord and Saviour

are brought by the Holy Spirit into one fully committed fellowship, holding the one apostolic faith, preaching the one Gospel, breaking the one bread, joining in common prayer, and having a corporate life reaching out into witness and service of all who, at the same time, are united with the whole Christian fellowship in all places and all ages in such wise that ministry and members are accepted by all, and that all can act and speak together as occasion requires for the task to which God calls His people. It is for such unity that we believe that we must pray and work.

Thus the Assembly came out with an official expression of the actual natural organic unity. What is needed in working toward this end is not merely an organization but a new spirit— a new willingness to share with one another as Christians and as churches—and a passionate desire to understand one another more deeply. In the theological discussions at New Delhi there was a new humility evident and at the same time a new boldness in trying to find one another; a new patience too, and a new insistence to penetrate in the analysis of each other's traditions to the point where at least a sympathetic and deep insight creates a bond of real mutual acceptance.

One of the important decisions of the New Delhi Assembly was the adoption of an addition to the present theological "basis" of the Council,

The World Council is a fellowship of churches which confess the Lord Jesus Christ as God and Saviour according to the Scriptures and therefore seek to fulfill together their common calling to the glory of the one God, Father, Son and Holy Spirit.

This new basis made many happy—the Lutherans because of the specific mention of scriptural authority; and the Orthodox by the clear pronouncement on the Trinity. However, in connection with the discussions leading to this new basis, many questions were asked as to the true nature and possible ecclesiological function of the WCC. There were some who hoped to increase the prestige of the WCC by giving it a new ecclesiological dignity, calling it a new "churchly reality." Dr. Franklin Fry, however, as the Chairman of the Central Committee, categorically stated that the total development of the ecumenical movement is "the most convincing refutation of the notion that the World Council is trying to build superchurch." The debate on the nature of the World Council and its future course, as New Delhi has shown, will greatly increase.

There are some who are particularly anxious to initiate a debate on the ecclesiological role of the Council. Dr. Truman B. Douglass, of the United Church of Christ, has been calling for a reappraisal of the councils by the denominations, feeling that "in our generation the dynamics of the ecumenical movement have burst its structural bonds." Dr. Douglass further emphasized that the constitutions of world, national and local councils (declaring a council strictly to be an instrument of the constituting churches) is no longer sufficient; further, that the councils are "to challenge the denominations in their complacent assumption that they alone are churches and rightly the object of their members' undivided loyalty." There is an equally strong demand among many of the pioneers of the conciliar movement to give the councils more freedom and authority and more prestige—possibly by declaring the councils to be equal in rank and dignity with the denominations.

To consider this trend and its objectives, let us look for a moment at the authoritative document. "The Church the Churches and the World Council of Churches" which was prepared and adopted by the central committee of the World Council of Churches at their meeting in 1950 in Toronto. The purpose of this document was to define the nature and role of the WCC. It clearly expresses what has been called by Dr. Douglass the "denominational presupposition," the assumption of the autonomy and the integrity of the denomination as the council's constituent members, the assumption that these member communions of the council are churches in the proper sense, and that the World Council is not to infringe on their authority or ever to attempt to attract the loyalty of the churches' individual members. The document clearly states that the Council is not to impose any thought pattern upon the churches. The Council is not even to have an opinion on what the unity of the churches ought to be, and is not to try to induce churches to get into discussions on unions and mergers. It is interesting that in this document the Council is always mentioned in connection with the things it is *not* to do while the paragraph on positive action always refers to the acting party as "the member churches" who will do "this" and "that" together. In a positive sense the Council is called the "fellowship of churches." In the introductory statement for this document it is clearly expressed that "the WCC is not a church, not an expression of the church, neither is it to be a nucleus of the coming great church. . . . The Council disavows any thought of becoming any single unified church . . . a structure independent of the churches . . . the Council is far from usurping any of the functions which already belong to its constituent churches. . . ." It disavows any intent to control the churches or to legislate for them and, indeed, is prevented by its constitution from doing so.

There are many of the active leaders of the conciliary movement who have felt that this document and the spirit behind it are actually making the Council into a mere slave of its masters, the denominations; that this "hemming in" of the Council has led to a decline of its significance, and in general to a dimming of the lights of conciliar ecumenicity. After having pleaded for decades the case that the churches should accept the ecumenical concern, many of the ecumenical leaders feel now after official acknowledgment of the movement has been allowed, the churches are exercising an intolerable control over it.

Two important proposals have been made recently to challenge this denominational presupposition of the World and National Council of Churches constitutions, and to exalt the role of the Councils quite beyond its present status. Dr. Truman Douglass demanded reappraisal of the denominations' relationship to the councils, particularly referring to the National Council of Churches. His complaint was that the churches and denominations "undervalue the significance of councils." He asserted "that the councils have outgrown and transcended their original relationship to their constituent members." Douglass protested against "the denominational presupposition," the idea that "since the denominations created the councils, that the denominations own them." "Councils," he continued, "are not the creatures of its constituents, but in some important sense they are called to be the judges of the denominations. They are to bring the denominations under scrutiny." This authority, according to Douglass, is not derived from the constituent members but from The Church of Christ which transcends all the churches.

Douglass derives his idea of an exalted authority of the Council from the fact that a council "bears witness to the full church and in a number of crucial points its witness is more faithful and more nearly adequate than that of the member denominations." Therefore, he wants the Council to become "an authority over the churches." He goes even so far as to speak of the Council as "becoming THE church in one of its modes; and in another sentence he describes the Council as "the church in exactly the form that is most uncomfortable for the churches." From here he sets out to attack the denominational presupposition, the uncritical assumption, that the denominations in their enterprises are proper objects of ultimate loyalty, the idea that what is good for the denominations is automatically good for the Kingdom of God. Douglass compares this attitude as displayed by the denominations with the taunting slogan, "what is good for General Motors is good for the Nation."†

Approaching the same problem another eminent ecumenical leader, Dr. Henry P. Van Dusen, President of Union Theological Seminary, arrives at similar conclusions. In an article, "Conciliar Ecumenicity and Church Union"* Van Dusen explores "this new form of churchly reality. Conciliary Association and its relationship to denominational structures which have come to us as legacy of the past Christian centuries." According to the sentiments expressed here somehow between

---

* *Christianity and Crisis,* Vol. XXI, No. 18, October 30, 1961.

† *The Christian Century,* Jan. 8, 1958.

the lines denominations are considered fitting structures of the past, but the present and the future demand a new churchly reality. Van Dusen asserts that the Council of Churches is not *the* Church but neither are the denominations *the* Church. He asks the question, by what right then do we deny a council to call and consider itself *a* church if we deem it proper to call denominations *a* church? According to Van Dusen the claim of a denomination to be a Church of Christ is based on three grounds; first, common history and tradition; second, common body of doctrine or creed; third, the ordaining of ministers and the administration of sacraments. Van Dusen sees no reason why councils could not fulfill these three conditions and thus become churches proper. As to the second of these vestiges of the church, he makes the rather astonishing statement, "there is a single finding that stands forth with indisputable clarity over more than two decades of ecumenical examination and debate regarding the creedal basis of our existing denominations, it is that in the basic issues of Christian belief (excepting only the doctrine of the church) there are no determinative differences." "Conciliary Association" is defined by Van Dusen "as the new churchly reality of Christian Community that has come to birth within Christendom in our own time and has been blessed by God with amazing growth and strength in these later years."

This trend to give the Council ecclesiological significance and to exalt it to a position above the denominations or equal to them should be carefully evaluated. I share Van Dusen's and Douglass's sense of concern about sluggishness in the ecumenical movement in our time. I also feel that the present design of the councils is inadequate for the task of prodding the churches to the goal of unity. And I am likewise aware that denominational particularism has gained new strength in these days, making the appeals of many denominational leaders for unity in our time sound hollow. Yet, I don't think that lifting the councils to ecclesiological heights will serve the progress of the ecumenical cause. The councils, by becoming churches, would become competitive with the denominations, and thus would be

impeded in carrying out their function as agencies of reconciliation among the churches. If the councils assume this new
ecclesiological posture, it will cause many of its constituent
members to leave them. In particular, a council which claims
to be a church or even the supreme manifestation of *the* Church
would make cooperation for the Eastern Orthodox, the Anglicans, the Lutherans, and other communions impossible; it
would also clearly foreclose any future possibility of including
the Church of Rome in ecumenical discussions of an official nature. In other words, the Council would no longer be a forum for
all the churches but would become an association of strictly
Protestant churches. There certainly is a place for a strong
movement with the restricted aim of straightening out the inner
Protestant dilemma, but this is not the central function of
the World Council of Churches or even the National Council.
There is no doubt that the denominations in our time are often
unbearably preoccupied with building up their own empire
rather than with making the one Church of Christ manifest to
the world, and it is the proper task of the councils to challenge
this denominational introversion. However, it is not this denominational self-idolization alone which stands in the way of
ecumenical fulfillment. To assume this would be to indulge in
an oversimplification. If there is fault with the denominations
there is equal fault with the councils, particularly the way in
which they have developed over the past years. The pioneers
of the conciliar movement tended to identify the unity of
Christ's Church with the accomplishment of their goal of
"conciliar association." But now that association has been
organizationally accomplished, many of the leaders of the
conciliar movement rightfully feel that the real unity of the
Church still evades us. Realizing this, should one not admit
that the dream of the conciliar movement was to an extent
illusory and even shallow? Should we not recognize that the
unity in Christ is first of all a spiritual matter—something
which must be grown and develop and cannot be achieved
primarily by organizational manipulation?

Many of the pioneers of the conciliar movement, often from

a Congregational background, seem to have fallen for the
Roman Catholic tendency of identifying the Church with its
institutional organizational aspects. As subjection under the
Pope constitutes and manifests church unity for the Catholics,
so the establishment of the World Council becomes for those
persons identical with accomplished church unity. This, however, is a form of thinking which will be unacceptable to
Protestants who understand the church primarily as the people
of God. Unless the people, in thought, understanding, and
willingness to share with one another, are really becoming one
in spirit, unity will still evade us in spite of all our inter-
relating of local, national, and world councils into a most impressive hierarchy. It is not my intention here to spiritualize
the concept of unity. On the contrary, I am quite convinced
that once spiritual unity emerges it must lead to organizational,
corporeal consequences. I do not shy away from the idea of
one united Church, one world Church as the eventual goal of
the ecumenical movement. But in our eagerness to make progress toward this goal we should be careful not to put the cart
before the horse.

Both Douglass and Van Dusen realize that after the demands of the conciliar movement have been established and
many of its basic goals accomplished, some important things
remain to be done. Unity is yet to be realized in fullness. Finding fault with the denomination, they are too uncritical of the
new agencies of unity themselves. They seem convinced that
once the present councils have been given new status, unity will
truly be ours. Unity is still thought of here in principle as the
result of organizational arrangements, yet with the added theological emphasis on "the new churchly reality" of conciliar
association. I feel strongly that the remedies suggested by Van
Dusen and Douglass will not be sufficient. More important, if
they are misunderstood, they might even worsen the patient's
condition. The remedy seems ineffective because it has been
prescribed on the basis of what to me seems an insufficient
diagnosis.

The optimism of the conciliar movement is based on the

assumption that there are in various Christian traditions no determinative differences and discrepancies in matters of faith. As a consequence there has been a tendency to belittle the question of truth and to sweep under the carpet some of the very obvious differences in the understandings of the biblical revelation. It is precisely this shallow optimism among some of the conciliar enthusiasts which has been an obstacle to further progress in deepening the mutual understandings among the Christian communions in matters of faith.

By establishing local national and world councils we have taken an important step toward unity; but unity has not yet been accomplished. We must, today, clearly realize that what we have so far done is only a first feeble step in the direction of unity; and that the councils as we have established them can be considered only as a preliminary scaffolding for a building yet to be erected. They are improvisations necessary, precisely, because of the divided status of the churches. They exist because of an ecclesiological malady. Their central function is to work toward understanding and reconciliation among the Christian churches by creating a climate of cooperative thinking and action in all member churches. This new trend to exalt the status of the Council seems to be based on the assumption that conciliar association is an end rather than a means.

Instead of working assiduously to achieve fellowship among the churches, many councils seem to accept the premise that such fellowship has already been accomplished, or that they aren't such fellowship and and that they can now go quietly about the business of building up their own organizations. No doubt the ever-increasing numbers of departments of city, national, and world councils fulfill many important tasks. But the question must still be asked, In what way does this activity contribute to the central task of the Council, which is to create greater unity among its constituents? The denominations have gone willingly along with the diffusion of the council's image into a multiple-purpose service agency. In fact, the churches seem at times to consider councils as agencies into whose lap they can dump all the undramatic tasks which they do not care to do themselves. There are members of the clergy who feel that someone ought to speak out prophetically on problems of social injustice. Yet in order not to alienate members of their own churches and not to expose themselves to undue criticism they like this task handled by a council.

Making the councils into service agencies and jacks-of-all-trades for the denominations has led to such organizational growth within the councils that to the individual Christian the council image appears as that of a more or less independent organization. There is no ready identification of the churches with the Council and certainly not of the individual Christian with the work of the Council. "The amazing growth" in many ways has only contributed to the popular image of the Council as an organization of its own, an entity in itself, the purpose of which is no longer clearly understood by the people. It is quite pathetic to see how little of the fine work that is done in the various departments of the National Council trickles down to the congregations and their individual members.

It is my contention that a radical change in the form of councils is necessary if we wish the councils to be effective instruments for bringing the churches together into a fellowship of churches. Rather than trying to become a Church, the Council should be eager to be only a council, working solely toward the achievement of a true fellowship among the churches. The councils should realistically accept their limitations and realize their full potential by being a forum of and for the churches. The Council's sole ambition should be to provide the possibility of rigorous and frank encounter and dialogue among its member churches—to create occasions of actual contact in study, dialogue, and fellowship in order to enhance mutual understanding—to achieve consensus and to reach unison in will and effort among its members. The essential element in all such efforts should be to provide occasion for the members to meet and to decide together rather than the Council acting for its members.

One development in particular has kept the councils from truly becoming the thinking and acting fellowship of churches. This is the fact that presently councils are often run by small policy committees who make all the important decisions. A sort of "guided democracy" is at work in councils—an expedient method in racing through incredibly long and utopian agendas, but a hindrance really in the process of common decision making.

Many delegates felt, and many expressed this privately at New Delhi, that the important decisions of the World Council are not really the decisions of the delegates but express the will and intention of powerful committees or some inner core of leaders. Too much of the time of the delegates is taken up by marching in and out, by listening to lectures, by participating in receptions and other representative occasions. And too little time is given for full-fledged debate in the Assembly prior to the decisions to be taken. The great decisions—as for instance, the merger of the International Missionary Council with the World Council of Churches—are not real decisions of the delegates of the Assembly.

It seems to me of paramount importance to give the plenary session of all delegates the place it deserves according to the constitution of the World Council. At present the various sections of the Assembly are presented with documents which have been prepared well in advance and which are to serve as the basis of the discussion. There is hardly any time even to discuss these documents sufficiently and there is considerable pressure to come out with resolutions after a few sessions. The result is that the final resolutions of the sections and of the whole Assembly often simply mirror the material fed to them in the first place.

I strongly feel that the present councils ought to be converted into true congresses of the churches—forums in which all the issues of great concern to the member churches—theological, ethical, practical—could be openly and passionately discussed. If there is one thing wrong with Protestant churches —and quite pathetically so—it is that they provide no leadership for its members. Here the Council—if it really were the place where all churches would send their wisest and ablest men—could fill a great void. It could provide the churches with an instrument to search for consensus and to reach a common commitment on principles and action. This would not be achieved just by authoritarian decrees which would be unacceptable to us and our understanding of the freedom of the Christian. But it would be achieved by a process which would allow for maximum participation of all the member communions in the decision-making process.

To outline how such effort could be realized, I would like to make the following proposal: an issue of real importance would be first discussed in congregational assemblies in the local churches—in thorough study and debate with an effort to reach a consensus within the congregation. The delegates of the congregation would then present the congregation's point of view at the local council's debate. The same issue would be further discussed within the denominational structures, diocese, presbyteries, and conferences, which, in turn, would present their opinions through their delegates at the regional council meetings. After this the issue at stake would be taken up by the National Council and finally by the World Council of Churches, if it were an issue of such a nature as to warrant world attention. If, after such a thorough process of lively and serious debate, beginning at the grass roots and carried finally to the attention of the World Council, resolutions would be made, then such resolutions would carry the "moral weight," to which they aspire. People would listen to them and be willing to identify themselves with these decisions and follow them. The regional and local councils, in turn, through their secretariats, could then see to it that the resolutions of the National or World Council would be made known and studied by the churches. No department of a council should make any resolutions of its own, but only contribute the result of its research and study to the full Council Assembly's discussion. And only the Assembly as a whole would reach final conclusions and issue resolutions.

The Assembly of the National and the World Council should meet once a year. To be a delegate of one's church to the National Council or World Council of Churches should be a full-time assignment over a period of years. To achieve the needed identification of our church members with the ongoing debate of the councils, the delegates should not just be appointed by the denominational heads, but rather be elected by vote by the broad membership of their denomination.

Instead of developing into monstrous bureaucracies lacking natural outlets for their efforts, the councils could thus become centers of contact and dialogue—places where Christians could talk with one another with utter frankness. There would be tension. There would be commotion. There would be suspense in these church congresses. But there would be life. And life always attracts the attention of people. Councils would be the places where Christians would search for truth together, seeking answers to our puzzling problems in the light of the Gospel. Councils then would fulfill a great mission by giving their member communions in our time a sense of direction in trying to achieve maximum unison of will and action in common obedience to our Lord. If national councils and the World Council will truly provide such leadership for its member churches then these councils will no longer have to worry about lacking authority.

In spite of all the optimism displayed by some conciliar association enthusiasts, we have through our ecumenical efforts only reached the state where churches begin to be polite to one another. But there is little communication or deep desire for sharing among the churches. Far from having solved the problem, disunity is still with us in all its ugly and shocking reality. If communication could truly be established, this would be a tremendous step toward the unity we seek. Councils, far from becoming bottlenecks of the ecumenical movement, would by their very nature and function be initiators of new motion toward unity.

TIME OF TESTING FOR THE NATIONAL COUNCIL

Henry P. Van Dusen

> *Henry P. Van Dusen* has the insight and experience equaled
> by few and excelled by none for evaluating the NCCC and the
> WCC. The President of Union Theological Seminary, New
> York, he has been intimately involved in the ecumenical move-
> ment both at home and abroad since his days as a student at
> Princeton and Edinburgh, and most recently served as Chair-
> man of the Joint Committee of the IMC/WCC which prepared
> for the integration of the two bodies.

*A*NY attempt to appraise The National Council of the
Churches of Christ in the United States of America as it is
today must be firmly placed and securely held within a context
of two recognitions. Both arise from its origins; but each holds
decisive importance for its present and its future. These recognitions constitute the determining background and framework
for whatever may be said about the National Council:

1. The achievement which the creation of the National Council of Churches USA represents, an achievement both
   unprecedented and awe-inspiring.
2. The role of this National Council within world ecumenical
   developments, a role at once unique and uniquely significant.

I

The National Council of Churches USA has been described as "beyond challenge, the most complex and intricate piece of ecclesiastical machinery which this planet has ever witnessed."

Few would be disposed to challenge that description. The only possible rival might be the supreme hierarchy of the Roman Catholic Church. But those who have lived and worked within the Vatican report that its operations are far less those of a mammoth monolithic structure which is often assumed than a congeries of largely autonomous and almost wholly uncoordinated offices which find such unity as they have through the ultimate responsibility of each to the Pope and his immediate advisers.

The complexity and intricacy of the National Council's organization were implicit in its process of formation. As is well known, it was brought into being through the merger of twelve (originally eight) previously independent interdenominational bodies, several of which had been in existence and had been developing their own complicated structures for more than half a century. One sympathetic interpreter declared that the National Council "is a merger and only a merger."

This was to be a "Council of Churches." Its membership was to consist of churches, not interdenominational agencies. Therefore, the proposal and the plan for its implementation had to be submitted to all the prospective member churches (29 at the time of the Constituting Convention; others joined later to constitute the present total membership of 31 churches). And each church had to take formal action of adherence.

But the Council was to be formed by the unification of 12 already existing agencies (later joined by several others). Each merging body, being itself interdenominational in character, had a numerous constituency of member organizations. For example, the Federal Council of Churches was composed of 27 denominations. The Foreign Missions Conference of North America represented 99 Mission Boards of 54 denominations. If we disregard for the moment the enormous membership of the church women, there were no fewer than 324 constituent members of the 12 merging bodies, to which the proposal and plan had to be submitted and whose ratification had to be in some fashion sought.

Moreover, each of the 12 merging bodies not only represented a numerous constituency. Each of them brought to the National Council its own internal structure of divisions, departments, boards, and committees, in some instances the result of fifty or more years of evolutionary development. All of these had to be provided for within the structure of the new National Council. The overwhelming bulk of the subsidiary elements within the merging bodies were incorporated unaltered and found their places in the structure of the National Council.

However, it is not altogether correct to say that the National Council is "a merger and only a merger" of previous organizational units and arrangements. To provide instrumentalities for consultation, coordination, and, in some instances, unification, in addition to the subsidiary elements in the merging bodies, a very considerable apparatus of interagency and all-Council units was devised and superimposed upon the already almost inconceivable complexities of the merger—General Departments, Central Departments, Central Bureau, Joint Departments, Joint Commission, Coordinating Committees. The Organizational Chart appended at the time of the Constituting Convention at Cleveland in 1950 set forth no fewer than 94 Boards, Departments, Bureaus, Commissions, and Committees.

If one's response to the creation of the National Council is one of admiration for the skill and statesmanship which brought it into being, one's reaction to its internal organization must be one of amazement at the ingenuity and imagination which elaborated its structure.

II

It is an accepted axiom of ecumenical history that almost every aspect and type of effort for and achievement of Christian unity began first and has advanced fastest and farthest in connection with Christian Missions; every aspect and type *except one*. With that single exception, the Christian World Mission has been both the precursor and the progenitor of the Movement for Christian Unity.

The effort to achieve Christian unity has gone forward in six phases which may be arranged in an ascending order of increasing significance:

  I. *Consultation*, for fellowship and mutual counsel.
 II. *Comity*, that is, agreement to divide responsibility and
       eschew overlapping and competition.
III. *Cooperation* in planning and action.
 IV. *Federation* in councils.
  V. *Confederation*, that is, unification of structure and re-
       sources for specific purposes and projects.
 VI. *Church union.*

Each of these six types of Christian unity has originated either in the work of Christian missions overseas or in the projection of Christian missions from the "home base"; each type of Christian unity has developed most rapidly within the missionary enterprise; each type has its most advanced and significant illustration today among the "younger churches," brought into existence by Christian missions in the past century and a half. Each type, *with one exception.*

I. It was a common conviction of missionary responsibility which first prompted Christians of different denominational affiliations to come together for *consultation*—the secretaries of four British missionary societies in London in 1819, and missionaries of four societies in Bombay in 1825.

II. The earliest recorded recognition of the obligation to effect Christian *comity*—"a high-sounding aphorism for avoidance of competition—which might perhaps more precisely be denominated "courtesy" was a resolution of the American Board of Commissioners for Foreign Missions in 1838.

III. The pioneering instance of *cooperation* in planning and action of individual Christians of different denominations was the epochal formation of the London Missionary Society in 1795.

IV. *Federation,* the creation of Church councils, or what is increasingly designated "conciliar ecumenicity." To be sure, even here there were anticipations on the mission field— federations or national missionary societies in the Philippines (1901), Japan (1902), India, Puerto Rico, and Korea (1905). We do not know whether these missionary pathfinders had a direct influence, at least by way of suggestion and example, upon the founders and architects of the Federal Council of Churches of Christ in America when they brought that body to birth in 1908. In any event, the Federal Council was the first formal association of denominational church bodies anywhere in the world for the prosecution of common tasks.

Whether or not the Federal Council was indebted to earlier precursors on the mission field, the germinative influence of the Federal Council upon the subsequent multiplication of this form of Christian unity is beyond question. The example of the American Federal Council has worked out across the face of the earth to inspire the formation of similar national federations or councils of churches to the present total of 68. Of these, 51 or exactly three-fourths are in "younger church" lands of Asia, Africa, Oceania, and Latin America. And the example of the American Federal Council has worked downward in the United States to prompt the proliferation of state, county, and local councils of churches to a total of almost a thousand. Similar councils are presently multiplying in cities and towns in unnumbered lands all over the world. Lastly, the Federal Council furnished the principal precedent and pattern for the World Council of Churches. In summary, the American Federal Council must be recognized as the pioneer and pace-setter of this form of Christian unity, councils or federations of churches, that is, conciliar ecumenicity. It is these facts which give its successor body, the National Council of Churches USA, a unique role in the chronicles of Christian unity.

Not only was the Federal Council the earliest instance of conciliar ecumenicity, but the National Council is today far and away the most elaborate and also the largest church council in the world. No other National Council of Churches or National Christian Council can begin to compare with it in size of staff, program or budget. And, in all these respects, it considerably surpasses the dimensions of the World Council of Churches:

| | *1962* | |
	Staff	*Budget*
World Council	202	$ 1,297,100
National Council, USA	650	15,414,110

V. *Confederation* refers to joint undertakings through which missions or mission boards or churches pool resources of personnel and finances in unified organizations for limited purposes or specific projects: "organic union—not, to be sure, of whole Church bodies—but of those Church bodies in their actual functioning in specific projects or areas." Probably the earliest was the Madras Christian College, transformed in 1876 into a union institution representing six denominations.

VI. In that expression of Christian unity which is usually regarded as climactic—*church union*—the earliest instance of the full and permanent unification of national churches drawn from different communions or church families was achieved in South India in 1908 by the merger of Congregational, Presbyterian, and Reformed bodies to create the South India United Church—one of the three constituents of the larger and vastly more significant Church of South India formed in 1947. Of the eighteen church unions across denominational barriers in Christian history, thirteen have occurred among younger Christian churches, including two of the three which by general recognition are the most noteworthy—the Church of South India and the Church of Christ in Japan.

Let it be said again, to the historical axiom that the varied types and forms of the multifarious effort for Christian unity originated within the Christian World Mission, there is a *single exception. It is federation, the creation of church councils, increasingly designated "conciliar ecumenicity."*

But how significant is "conciliar ecumenicity" in the larger cause of Christian unity?

It is of utmost importance to recognize that the Christian Council or Council of Churches, of which the National Council of Churches USA is both the earliest and largest illustration, is something genuinely *new* in Christendom, without precedent or even anticipation in the first eighteen centuries of Christian history.

We must not be misled by similarity of *name* to the so-called "ecumenical councils" of the early centuries. In no significant sense were they analogous to, or forerunners of, the councils of churches of today. They were occasional assemblages of groups of bishops, seldom adequately representative of the whole of Christendom of that day, brought together to wrestle with specific current issues, usually conflicts over heresy or ecclesiastical authority. In sound historic perspective, they appear as predominantly sectional or regional conclaves of embattled ecclesiastics engaged in largely ineffectual efforts to secure and maintain theological uniformity and thus heal divisions or avert schisms. The main point is: they contemplated and provided no continuing instrumentalities for consultation, let alone for united action.

In contrast, the Council of Churches is a new form of church life. It constitutes a wholly original development and one of the most important within or of the Body of Christ since the Day of Pentecost. Its *theological* significance has hardly begun to be explored. In the judgment of some, it constitutes one of the two alternative forms in which the ultimate ideal unity of Christ's Church may be conceived, the other being the form which heretofore has been almost universally assumed to be the goal—*Church union.*

In the light of these facts, the significance of the future of the National Council of Churches USA looms large.

III

In December, 1962, the National Council of Churches completed 12 years of existence. What has more than a decade of experience revealed regarding this body, whose creation represented such a remarkable achievement, whose future holds such importance for the cause of Christian unity?

This essay is concerned solely with questions which are being widely canvassed by critically minded participants and friends. They are principally in four areas:

1. The adequacy of the structure and procedures of the Council as originally conceived and as actually functioning today.
2. The effectiveness of the present operation of the Council as the corporate agency of its member churches.
3. The possibility of free and prophetic initiative and influence within so vast and complicated an ecclesiastical institution.
4. The present and potential role of this Council within ecumenical Christianity.

From the outset, many of the most ardent and devoted supporters of the National Council, confronted with the multifarious complexities of its organization, have forecast that the day would come when a thorough overhauling and reordering of its structure would be mandatory. Not a few are suggesting that that time is now.

Such a proposal does not necessarily imply criticism of the original plan. Merely to join 12 well established, fully functioning bodies, most of them with already highly articulated patterns of internal organization, inevitably foreordained an elaborate framework. As the implications of merger appeared, the necessity of providing for instruments of interrelationship among the uniting bodies was apparent. Seemingly, the method followed was: wherever such a need appeared, to create a new agency to meet it. Hence the multiplication of general, central, joint departments, and so forth.

Nor does such a proposal envision a conventional "streamlining" procedure, after the fashion so favored in American business circles, with threatened loss of individuality, flexibility, and adaptability, if not strait-jacketing within too logical and rigid forms. In so vast an enterprise, maximum decentralization with utmost autonomy is highly desirable. Nevertheless, some degree of simplification is clearly overdue.

The World Council of Churches, which came into being with less than a score of subsidiary units, was bold enough to undertake a radical recasting of its main structure between its first and second assemblies. One result was: its dozen program departments were unified into four divisions.

At the meeting of the National Council's General Board in June, 1962, a first step was taken to initiate a comprehensive self-examination of structure looking toward possible reconstruction. Pending the outcome of this process, it must suffice to underscore its urgency and express a fervent hope that the resulting proposals will be bold, imaginative, comprehensive, and far-reaching. They should be informed and determined by a passion for simplicity, directness and effectiveness rather than by the all-too-familiar American penchant for elaboration, multiplication, and consequent "complification," a penchant from which, some have felt, the officers of the Council have not been wholly free.

However, something far more fundamental and drastic than a mere reshuffling of institutional machinery should be explored, devised, and implemented. What is needed is nothing less than a stringent scrutiny of the entire prevailing pattern of procedures by which the National Council, acting through the triennial meetings of its General Assembly and the semiannual sessions of the latter's interim body, the General Board, presently functions.

In the current triennium, the voting participants in the General Assembly total 809, in the General Board 276 (101 of the latter exercising a fractional vote). Both bodies operate very much after the fashion of conventional American "democratic legislatures." It cannot be said that they are more cumbersome, confused, tedious, and ineffectual than similar organs of comparable size, whether political or ecclesiastical.

A more basic query may be pressed as to whether *political* devices constitute sound patterns for *churchly* organs. There is a clamant need for fresh, original, and fearless thinking as to *how* a representative *Christian* organism should order its life and its ways of fulfilling its responsibilities, with conclusions which might well dictate deep-going and daring departures from traditional methods and patterns of behavior.

Here is a pressing imperative not only for the National Council of Churches USA. At the New Delhi Assembly of the World Council of Churches, so largely patterned on the National Council, a considered conclusion was voiced by many that the World Council must not enter its next Assembly without a no less painful self-scrutiny and drastic recasting of procedures.

If such reform should be explored with respect to the Assemblies of both World and National Councils, it is even more mandatory in the case of their respective interim bodies, the Central Committee and the General Board. As I have elsewhere reported regarding the World Council: "A number of the most faithful and valued members of the policy-determining Central Committee confess privately their deepening concern and apprehension over what they believe to be an increasing formalism, conservatism and unreality in the Central Committee's procedures from year to year."* Some who have participated also in the National Council's General Board voice a like misgiving.

Unhappiness over the functioning of the General Board is at the basic level: the items which preoccupy its agenda and

* Cf. *One Great Ground of Hope: Christian Missions and Christian Unity,* (Westminster Press, 1961), *passim.*

which, presumably, reflect what is supposed to claim its attention and what it is expected to accomplish. This is revealed in
the material furnished to the members of the General Board
in preparation for its meetings. Not infrequently, this consists
wholly in lengthy and often highly technical draft statements
which come up to it from one to another of its multitudinous
constituent units and which it is expected to scrutinize and
approve as formal pronouncements of the National Council.
The impression made upon the mind of the conscientious Board
member is that these documents will comprise the business of
the Council; in any event, they embrace all that he is asked to
prepare for.

The elemental query is: what purpose is the Board expected
to fulfill, to what matters should it give major attention, where
if at all is there provision, indeed anticipation, of creative thinking and bold and truly significant action?

The concern which appears to preoccupy the National Council's officers themselves at the present time is not unrelated to
what has just been said. It is prompted by disquiet as to the
present effectiveness of the Council in relationship to and as
agent of its member churches. In one perspective, it is the question: how can the National Council better serve the churches?
But in the obverse and more disturbing perspective, it is: how
can the churches be lured into more active and significant participation in the life and program of *their* National Council?

The Council's officers have been led to an approach to this
dual question which is as sound as it is shrewd—to pose the
issues of mutual relationship and involvement within a far
broader and profounder perspective: what is the normative role
of the American churches in their nation and the world in the
present era? What are the major tasks to which they *should be*
devoting major attention and effort? and then, where and how
should the National Council (and also state and local Councils
of Churches) be involved in their discharge? It is proposed that
these elemental and caustic questions be faced by the member
churches and their Councils *together* through a wide-ranging

(and perhaps protracted) process of joint inquiry and consultation under the caption: LONG RANGE PLANNING.

In the perspective of this essay, the heart of the matter is the question of *leadership*. Do the churches desire and expect the National Council to lead them?

This question strikes to the core of the *raison d'être* as well as the program of the National Council of Churches. No profession has been more often reiterated by National Council spokesmen than that the Council is "the servant of the churches." By many this has been interpreted to mean that the Council, as the creature of its member churches, should aspire to be no more than their reflection and mouthpiece. Some have felt that its officers characteristically manifest a caution bordering on timidity.

The same issue was faced by the World Council at its New Delhi Assembly. The result was a forthright declaration that an ecumenical Council can truly serve the churches only as it makes bold to attempt to *lead* the churches:

> The World Council sees itself called not only into the tide of events but to be ahead of them, and recommends that this should be the continued aspiration of the Council. It feels that the Council should give its member churches spiritual and practical guidance in a Christian approach to the actual questions and problems of our day, such as materialism, secularism, peace and war, social justice, etc. The WCC should certainly not wait to be pushed into critical situations, but should always take the lead and initiative in asking "What is the commandment of Our Lord in the present time?"

There are not a few who are persuaded that here is the central, the decisive issue for the immediate future of conciliar ecumenicity: should a Council, whether world or national, merely reflect and obey, or is it called to lead? Implicit in that question is the theological issue of the nature of a "Council"—"the ecclesiological significance of councils of churches."

If one were asked to isolate and define the issue which more than any other, perhaps more than all others together, will in the end of the day determine the future of ecumenical Christianity, its profound and enduring influence or its ephemeral and importance, strange to say, it would not be difficult to fulfill the assignment. It is the issue of *leadership*. But the issue is a dual one; it can be put in two inter-related questions:

1. Will the churches look to the councils—whether local, national, or world—to lead them?
2. Will the councils be able to command for *their* leadership, not only as representatives of the churches but as full-time professional staff members, the ablest, most far-visioned, prophetic, deeply dedicated, Christlike leaders out of all the churches?

Affirmative answers to both questions are *sine qua non* for advance in Christian unity. Unless the councils can draft for their leadership—not only as official representatives of the churches but also, and far more determinative, as full-time professional staff members—the most gifted, dedicated and influential leaders of the churches, there is no possibility that the churches will look to the councils to lead them; and contrary-wise. *But*—this may be hard doctrine but its logic is inescapable—if the churches are not prepared to surrender to the councils for staff leadership their own foremost leaders—bishops, presidents, stated clerks, superintendents, theologians, and so on—it is clear proof of the role which the churches in fact assign to Christian unity, a secondary role. It is concrete confirmation of what Dr. Truman Douglass has called the "denominational presupposition" but might more properly be named the "denominational heresy"—that "the denomination and its enterprises are proper objects of ultimate loyalty," and therefore rightly retain their ablest personnel for their own leadership.

Among some of the National Council's friendliest well-wishers, misgiving lies at what they believe to be a still deeper and more fundamental level. It is a misgiving which is felt not alone with respect to the American National Council, but hardly less with respect to the World Council. It is the query whether far-visioned prophetic and daring initiative can have full and effective expression within a body which is not only so mammoth in size but, more important, which is firmly anchored within formal and conventional ecclesiastical structures.

With respect to the National Council, this query began to be voiced within a year of the Council's launching. Dr. John C. Bennett in *Christianity and Crisis* for January 7, 1952, posed the question, "Whither the National Council?"

The National Council of Churches has been in existence for a year. It is too early to say what it may become but it is perhaps fitting to call attention to several dangers which have emerged. . . . The chief danger consists in the possibility that the prophetic leadership of the churches, which was one of the great contributions of the Federal Council of Churches, may not be allowed to appear in the new structure. . . .

In a subsequent issue of the same journal (May 12, 1952), Dr. Eugene Carson Blake, who later became President of the National Council, replied to Dr. Bennett, recognizing the validity of his misgiving, but balancing it with a counterconcern "that the new National Council listen to and heed not only the voices of the prophets among us, but also the voices of wise men and practical who do not always agree with the prophets . . . I am as fearful of the arrogance of the liberal as I am of the machinations of the conservative."

In a still later issue (July 7, 1952) I ventured to raise the question: "Are the sins of liberals and conservatives equally blameworthy?" And then I went on to suggest:

The Ecumenical Movement, in both its American and World organs, stands today at a moment of fateful transition, marked by transfer of responsibility for its direction out of the hands of a relatively small group of men, mostly of pioneering vision and spirit, into the hands of a very much larger number of denominational officials and spokesman, many of them by temperament and habit cautious and conservative, who had a minor part in the creation of the Movement but must now guide its future. . . . Whether this transition can be effected without the by-product which has accompanied so many similar transitions in Christian history . . . the quiet and gradual but firm elimination of the prophets . . . remains to be seen.

The issue of prophetic conciliar leadership has reappeared from time to time in the ecumenical discussions through the past decades. It was the subject of vigorous debate at the annual meeting of the United States Conference for the World Council of Churches at Buck Hill Falls in April, 1960. That debate was initiated by a provocative paper by one of the editors of this volume, the Reverend Walter D. Wagoner, who laid down the premise:

> The World Council, through no egregious fault of its own, is now subject to the same transitional tensions, dangers, and opportunities which confront any worthy movement after the days of its youth. It is becoming more institutionalized, more settled in its ways. And although the WCC is not a church, it does face the same sociological and morphological pressures and patterns as do all new churchly movements.

Substitute for "WCC" the initials "NCCUSA," and all that Mr. Wagoner said applies almost equally and trenchantly to our inquiry.

Although it is doubtful whether the issue has been wrestled with explicitly in just these terms by the architects of either the World or the National Council, each organization has in fact recognized it and attempted to resolve it in their operative procedures. The World Council has continued the device of one of its two parent bodies, the Universal Christian Council for Life and Work, by generous employment of the "principle of co-option" in the persons of "consultants" or "advisers"; and it has opened membership on its commissions and committees, which initiates most of its program, to persons chosen for their special competence who are not appointees of the Member-Churches although their appointment must be approved by their churches. The National Council USA has also followed the latter procedure; and the large membership of its General Board has opened the possibility for denominations to include

some younger and "prophetic" spirits among their official representatives. Nevertheless, church officials tend to dislike and
distrust the "principle of cooption" or consultants. And, since
they constitute the core of the official membership of church
councils, they are always in a position to negate the influence
of bolder and more progressive individuals, or to tether or even
silence them.

The central issue is: the role of independent, progressive,
and sometimes radical individuals and groups within movements which are predominantly ecclesiastical in structure and
control. Obviously, this is the age-old tension between the
"prophetic" and the "priestly" elements within the Church of
Christ. The overarching question is: can ecumenical Christianity
learn the manifest lesson of Christian history and be bold enough
to insist that this tension shall *not* be resolved—almost always
in the past through the dominance of the ecclesiastical and the
suppression or emasculation of the prophetic . . . but, rather,
that the testing and painful tension shall be deliberately main-
tained by provision within the Council of Churches for equal
influence by both wings of the Church?

The final word must be a return to a reiteration of the pe-
culiar role which, in the providence of God, has fallen to the
National Council. As pioneer and pathfinder of conciliar
ecumenicity, and as today the largest and in some respects
the strongest Council of Churches in the world, unique importance attaches to its future. It would be quite untrue to
suggest that the eyes of the Christian world are fastened upon
that development. But, just as contemporary church historians
recognize the emergence of the Council of Churches in its earliest
and most elaborate expression in the United States as an event
of immeasurable importance in the history of Christendom, so
it is not beyond the range of possibility that future historians
will look back upon the further evolution of the National Council as one of the determinative factors in the life of Christ's
Church in the second half of the twentieth century.

UNITY AND THE SOUND BARRIER

CAN UNITY BEGIN AT HOME?

William B. Cate

William Cate is Executive Secretary of the Greater Portland Council of Churches in Oregon. The ecumenical bluff has "to be called" on Main Street and this Methodist minister offers a plan for doing it.

*A*NY discussion of Christian unity on Main Street today must take its bearings from the "New Delhi Assembly Statement on Unity" which was approved by the Third Assembly of the World Council of Churches at New Delhi, India, December, 1961. This statement is viewed by Christian leaders in many local communities as a mandate to explore new and creative forms of local Christian unity.

The heart of the statement declares, "We believe that the unity which is both God's will and His gift to His Church is being made visible as all in each place who are baptized into Jesus Christ and confess him as Lord and Saviour are brought by the Holy Spirit into one fully committed fellowship, holding the one apostolic faith, preaching the one Gospel, breaking the one bread, joining in common prayer, and having a corporate life reaching out in witness and service to all and who at the same time are limited with the whole Christian fellowship in all places and all ages in such wise that ministry and members are accepted by all, and that all can act and speak together as occasion requires for the tasks to which God calls his people."

The Local Ramifications of the
New Delhi Assembly Statement on Unity

What does this statement convey to Main Street, USA, about Christian unity? First of all, it says that we must resolve the serious theological issues that separate the church at its very heart, such as the sacraments, the nature and authority of the ministry, and the nature of the church. These issues cannot be passed by lightly as the sole responsibility of the ecclesiastical leaders and theologians in the denominations. Clergymen and laymen in the local communities are committed to wrestling with these areas of misunderstanding that stand in the way of a fully committed fellowship in each place.

Secondly, the implications of the phrase in the statement, "having a corporate life reaching out in witness and service," should be fully explored. For instance, we see here an impetus for the churches to take seriously their pastoral responsibility for the total life of the community. Dr. J. Quinter Miller in his excellent book *Christian Unity, Its Relevance to the Community* says, "a principal contribution of the churches to community is to nurture the vision and idealism of the community, and to vitalize that spiritual aspiration that gives to life its true quality. The character of the citizens of the community depends on this spiritual nurture. But the divisive character of Protestantism, unassisted by the conciliar process, often leaves the community impoverished because it receives no adequate spiritual nurture." It has been very difficult for the divided church to serve as an instrument in projecting the power of the Christian gospel into the social fabric of urbanized America.

It is apparent that the divided Christian Church not only fails to relate itself effectively to the community, but that the present denominational structure of the church contributes to the disintegration of the life of a community. By its inherent organizational nature the denominational approach is divisive in a community rather than integrative. In America the council of churches movement presents itself as an institutional effort in the church to correct this inherent problem in the denominational structure.

In the local community a serious attitude toward the churches' responsibility for the community means that divided Christendom must cast aside its own institutional ends and begin planning together the total mission of the church. The new emphasis on planning among the churches can be the means or process through which separate and autonomous religious groups are able to plan together the mission of the church to the community. In the past it has been traditional for each denominational group to plan according to its limited view of the task of the church and its marginal understanding of its responsibility to meet the religious needs of the community. Planning means that we look at the religious needs of the community together and then project our plans of outreach to meet this need.

Thirdly, the New Delhi Statement on Unity implies that local communities must become laboratories for social engineering in new forms of church structure. We cannot assume that the structure of our denominations or councils of churches will go unchanged in any given period of time. It must be realized that they should be radically modified as the dictates of the Gospel and of human need require. The operating thesis must be that structure should always follow function.

Finally, the New Delhi Statement on Unity makes imperative renewed efforts to establish full communication between all segments of Christendom. Owing to the impact of many present events of history dialogue is increasing among Protestants, Orthodox and Roman Catholics. One of the reports at the 1961 Pacific Northwest Faith and Order Conference stated concerning historic Protestant and Evangelical (fundamentalist) tensions, "There is a more recently felt softening of these differences, and some beginnings of conversations in local ministerial associations, and cooperation in life and work concerns." These relations are improving but they still represent a great scandal in the Protestant fellowship.

In order that we might chart more concrete steps for unity and mission on Main Street it is imperative to know where road-blocks and limitations now exist. Christian unity seems to be forging ahead with great strides on the world and national levels. Why is it not growing more rapidly on Main Street?

There are two primary factors in the life of the church today that impede the grassroots desire for unity and effective outreach of the church into the life of the community on Main Street. The first and basic factor is the unmodified continuance of the rigid denominational structure of the church which thwarts in many ways the grassroots desire for unity and mission. The second factor is the present image of their task held by many local councils of churches.

Limitations in the Denominational Pattern of the Church

In what way does the denominational pattern of church life impede unity and mission on Main Street? First, the denominational pattern of the church is not a functional organizational aid in helping the local church to meet the religious needs of a modern urban community. The denominational structure does not help the local church relate effectively to the power structures and social institutions of the city. For example, the public communications media such as television will offer free public service time only to a common instrument of the churches such as a council of churches to avoid being drawn into a competitive hassle with numerous denominations, each seeking an advantage for itself. If the church is to play a reconciling or a prophetic role in a community issue, those involved must feel that this is Christ's Church at work and not some fragmentary, sectarian body. The community wants to relate to the whole church, not a splinter portion of it.

The denominational organization of the church does not seem to infuse a proper sense of community responsibility into its churches. This failure is largely attributable to its structure. Customarily a denomination is not oriented to a particular city or community. Its main responsibility is the welfare of its local churches in various communities rather than the assumption of total Christian responsibility for the life of any particular community. It is not that many denominational leaders, or even clergy, have no interest in these things. It is simply that they do not quite feel that the responsibility for accepting this total concern is theirs.

In the Home Missions study book, *Edge of the Edge,* Theodore E. Matson points out that most Protestant local churches in the city are self-oriented, institutionally minded fellowships rather than parish-, neighborhood-, or community-oriented churches. Urban churches increasingly obtain their parishioners from all areas of the city because of the ease of modern transportation. There has resulted a decline in any special responsibility for a clearly defined parish or neighborhood. H. Richard Niebuhr pointed out in a lecture to an assembly of council of churches executives that the only sociological phenomenon with which the divided, competing churches can be compared to in America is that of gasoline stations with their different brands of gasoline to peddle to prospective clients.

A resulting failure of the church on Main Street has been the obvious neglect of the disinherited or the unprofitable clients of the community. The average self-oriented Protestant Church, except in rare cases, does not seem to know how to project itself beyond its own four walls to express compassion to the drug addict, alcoholic, and those alienated people who are adrift in the world separated from God and man. Unfortunately, it has been the pattern of most churches to relegate this institutionally unprofitable work to the little gospel missions upon whom they bestow a small contribution and thereby ease their conscience.

The assertion being made here is that the persistence of rigidity in the denominational structuring of the church is to a great extent responsible for the distortion of the local church into an increasingly parochial, self-oriented, and isolated institution in the local community.

On the world and national church level, the denominational drag is not felt as severely as in the local community. Here the councils of churches are working with the world and national staffs or as they have been termed, the administrative power groups of the denominations. Some national ecclesiastical leaders have been known to be most cooperative on this plane so long as their denominational programs are not disrupted in the local community.

The relentless propaganda and organizational drive upon the local church from the administrative power groups in most denominations is a major disruptive factor in the effort to increase unity on Main Street. This is especially so in the promotion of the program of the various denominational boards. Denominational programming has as its aim to aid the local church in carrying out its basic function as a church. The bureaucratic thrust of the programming boards, which have increased measurably in the last few years, has also, in part at least, the purpose of making itself indispensable to the life of the local church. It must be recognized that every denominational structure must have social control or discipline to maintain stability in the structure. This social control, which is necessary to institutional health, becomes a stumbling block to Christian unity in the local community when it is used to protect the programming function of the denomination at the expense of any effort toward comprehensive planning of the mission of the church by the churches on Main Street.

The most serious indictment of the denominational structure of the church is that it finds little real loyalty or theological justification in the belief of the laity and, for that matter, among many of the clergy. It is the rare denominational structure that affords confessional loyalty. Ecclesiastical structure no longer relates to specific theological orientation.

The misfortune is not that there is a disenchantment about the theological justification for our denominational structures. The tragedy is that little of the new biblical and ecumenical understanding of the church has sifted down into the local church to fill this vacuum. The clergy, as a whole, do not think theologically about the church. They have no clear image of the new shape the church should take. They are, therefore, un-sheltered victims of environmental pressures that force the church, increasingly, to conform to secular concepts rather than to more constraining, theological images of the church.

Consequently it is no surprise that there is so little motiva-tion for unity or mission from a Christian perspective in the local church. Clergy and laity alike rarely have a clear image of the mission upon which they are embarked. The laity do feel an inexplainable lack of reality in much of the work and worship of the local church. They sense that the church is stalled in an eddy and is not navigating in the mainstream of history.

If there is to be a renewal of the church, theological awaken-ing must begin in the local church. One of the important ways awakening comes is from confrontation with conflicting theologi-cal views. In the past, theological discussion among Christians was felt to be dynamite that should not be touched or, as in many cases, there was so little theological interest that a healthy discussion of basic matters of the faith could not take place. Fortunately, since the 1957 North American Faith and Order Conference at Oberlin, Ohio, there has been the growing convic-tion that faith and order discussion on Main Street is as basic to the realization of fuller unity as life and work activity.

Are Councils of Churches Contributing to Unity?

After properly scourging the denominational pattern of the church for its inadequacies, it is fitting to ask how well councils of churches are contributing to unity on Main Street. Councils of churches are the institutional form that much of the ecu-menical movement has taken in the United States. As intimated earlier in this paper, the denominational approach to the local community has been softened but not corrected by the work of the World Council and the National Council of Churches. In fact, it is a legitimate question to raise as to whether or not the council of churches movement on the national level has not tended, unknowingly, to confirm, strengthen, and perpetuate the denominational approach to the local community. The ecumenical encounter has affected some groups with a softening of attitude, other groups have reacted to the encounter with an aroused denominational self-awareness and resultant rigidity of impact in the local community. The council movement on the national level has been a strengthening factor in the life of the denominations and to that degree has perpetuated the divisive pattern of church life.

The weakness of local councils of churches as instruments for unity has been their tendency to be an activity oriented organization absorbed only with life and work concerns. As an upshot, councils of churches are often guilty of merely reflecting the state of the church in a local community instead of representing the means of creative theological ferment and drawing on ecumenical theological insight that transforms the church into more accord with the mind of her Lord.

Much of the activity that takes place in many councils of churches does not contribute appreciably to the growth of ecumenical understanding. It must be said that the ecumenical contacts that people have at union worship services such as at Easter, Holy Week, Reformation Day, Choir Festivals, to name a few events, do little to contribute to Christian unity except on a very superficial level. Participation in a service of a particular Christian tradition is much more helpful than these watereddown lowest-common-denominator interchurch events.

It is also true that many people can work at social action projects or Christian education activities in a council of churches and never be confronted with the scandal of division or the Biblical imperative to manifest Christ's Church as one unfragmented body. Members of a council of churches composed largely of the central core Protestant groups may be so likeminded that they never run into any basic theological conflicts. The entrance of the Episcopal Church, the Lutherans, and the Orthodox into local church council life has contributed much to highlighting the real issues that separate the churches and has begun to lead the churches to a reevaluation of the nature of the church.

Councils of churches are usually relegated the unprofitable areas of program. Many council leaders complain that whenever they create something of value, such as an effective leadership training program, youth work, observation schools, and the like, the denominations take it over. Many council leaders feel themselves as little more than "ecclesiastical errand boys" for the denominations and not leaders of institutions dedicated to the renewal and the reunion of the church.

J. Quinter Miller refers to the representative principle as being the key to effective council organization. "A council of churches so constituted," he states, "is the representative agent of its member congregations." This is a basic organizational concept and any council executive who violates it will be the sadder for it. To assume, however, that the task of a council of churches is to be only "the voice" of its member churches is a fatal mistake for Christian unity. A local council of churches must engage the churches in theological conversation concerning the biblical images of the church and work arduously at the theological differences that separate the fellowship of the church. A council of churches must bring a prophetic and challenging dimension into the life of the churches of a community.

Why have not local councils of churches better carried out this task? It is because many do not understand the faith and order dimension as being a basic responsibility of local council leadership. More than one council executive has told this writer that he did not see faith and order concerns as a part of his responsibility of leadership in his council of churches. It must be observed that many council executives are seemingly transplanted denominational people without any special training or commitment to any kind of ecumenical transformation of the church. Leadership in any organization limits what can be done. Many denominations still make it vocationally difficult for some of their most highly qualified young men to become church council executives.

The neglected role of local councils of churches in America, and this has been true of the state and the National Council of

Churches as well, has been that of theological encounter through faith and order involvement. Ecumenical understanding occurs when real meeting takes place between isolated brethren. Life and work activity, while creating a milieu for this meeting, is but preparation for real encounter. The common search for the nature of our unity brings the transforming light of the scriptural and theological insight into the life of the churches.

When faith and order and life and work are kept in proper balance in a local council of churches the council becomes a means to unity, a place of creative dialogue re-forming the churches' institutional patterns, not simply a makeshift vehicle of limited interaction through marginal cooperation which stagnates the ecumenical movement into a holding organization for its member units.

Active cooperation on practical tasks in a council of churches must often be by necessity limited, but encounter in faith and order concerns can include all Christendom. We can always talk. It has been the experience of the author that faith and order dialogue with the most divergent Christian groups opens up new areas of cooperative practical activity. Whereas, life and work prepares for faith and order, the pattern can also be turned about.

The fundamental role of a council of churches on Main Street is to create unity among the churches. It is not simply another programming unit in the church. However, a purpose concomitant with unity is the utilization of a local council of churches as a vehicle of the outward mission of the church. On Main Street, the local council's most significant role in mission is to be the catalyst between church and community. This means becoming the vehicle through which Christian values are transmitted into the fabric of a community. Councils in the past have often been guilty of simply tinkering with a few marginal and traditional moral issues. At a recent gathering of council executives, reports were made on the most significant occurrences in each council in the past year. More than 50 percent of the reports dealt with some cooperative Christian ventures dealing with liquor problems in the community or with racetrack and gambling issues. These prevalent evils, it is widely recognized, are only the results in our culture of more basic spiritual problems.

More important for a local council of churches is the need to begin creative study of ways whereby the church can enter into dialogue with society at its core. As in the area of the realization of unity, the church cannot communicate the Gospel unless there is meeting. A council of churches as a catalytic agent can place, for instance, in a Christian Social Concerns Commission the responsibility of the church to express the church's message of judgment or reconciling love into areas of concern and conflict in the community. In Portland, Oregon, the old method of standing off and making statements about social evils has been replaced by a consultative method. This new approach is simply that of bringing Christian concern and insight to situations embroiled in conflict or on the verge of conflagration by means of talking over the problem with the people involved and helping them work out a solution. Great success has met the efforts in Portland in race problems, civic issues, and interfaith conflict by using this approach. Most important is the image of the church that is conveyed. The consultative approach develops the image of the church as that of the servant rather than that of the noninvolved purist advising from afar.

This writer looks to the day when enough unity will be realized so that all the churches in a community can sit down together and, in the light of relevant theological and sociological facts viewed from various religious perspectives, begin to plan the total mission of the church for Main Street. This kind of unity does not depend upon any rigid, uniform organizational structure for the churches in a community. It does necessitate a commitment to Christian unity and the freedom of the churches in their denominational family relationships to plan together with other churches for a total ministry to the entire community. Planning can be the process through which the churches are led to the fuller unity set forth in the New Delhi Assembly Statement on Unity.

THE CINDERELLAS OF THE MOVEMENT

Robert Paul

Robert Paul was a parish minister in England before joining the World Council staff at the Ecumenical Institute at Bossey. He is now Professor of Church History at the Hartford Seminary Foundation in Hartford, Connecticut.

THE parish minister has become the Cinderella of the Ecumenical Movement at both the theological and at the practical levels; and yet we have reached a point in the history of the movement where it cannot go much further until it has enlisted the devotion and commitment of ministers in their parishes.

A few months after the Amsterdam Assembly in 1948 there was a large meeting in the Central Hall, Westminster, in which a former Bishop of London (Dr. J. W. C. Wand) declared that the most important task left for the delegates to accomplish was to see that the message and meaning of Amsterdam reached the parishes. As far as I know that never happened in England, and I have a shrewd suspicion that it has not happened elsewhere. For the key to the parish is the parish minister or priest, and in the minds of a good many ministers in the parishes the Ecumenical Movement is almost exclusively the concern of the Church's privileged classes—the administrative hierarchy, the theologians and scholars, and that select number among the laity whom the Church delighteth to honor.

In almost every ecumenical conference where people become vocal, someone is bound to raise a question about the inadequate representation of the laity, but no one, as far as I know, has ever raised the plea that the denominations should appoint more full-time parish ministers as their representatives; and that is not surprising, for by and large the parish ministers are not present in the conferences where they might make their protest.

However the question is not simply one of parish ministers being more adequately represented in the delegations that find their way to high-powered conferences. The issue becomes most acute at the theological level, in the concept of the Church that is emerging out of ecumenical discussion, and particularly in the place which the minister should occupy within such a Church.

Theological Uncertainty

Some time ago *The New York Times* reviewed the recent decline in the number of recruits for the Christian ministry. The writer suggested that the situation was in part owing to the fact that science demands the same kind of self-dedication and discipline that were once the proud and exclusive prerogatives of the classical professions, but he also added the suggestion that the Church's recent teaching about the laity has backfired. The implication is that the new concentration upon a "theology of the laity" has enabled some potential candidates to justify their evading the claims of the ministry. They argue, so the writer would suggest, that if they can still be a full-time servant of the Lord in any profession, and still earn their $15,000 a year, why should they (apparently) do no more for the Gospel, but earn much less for themselves, by entering the ranks of the clergy?

One of the greatest contributions of the Ecumenical Movement in recent years has been a new theological appreciation of what it means to be a lay Christian within the Church. It arose out of the rediscovery of the Church by its members, and the rediscovery of members by the Church itself, during the dark days of Nazi occupation in Europe—out of the whole movement which produced the evangelical academies and the Kirchentag. It was voiced by Bishop Stephen Neill at Amsterdam. The ecumenical dimensions of the issue came to Protestants with something of a shock when they read the works of Roman Catholics like Yves Congar, Gérard Philips, and J. M. Perrin, and nothing has contributed more to this theological reassessment of the place of the laymen in the Church and the world than the publications of the World Council of Churches' Department for the Laity and the insights of its former Secretary, Hans Ruedi Weber. The result has been to give the informed layman a new dignity in relation to the Church and its witness that is surely true to the Bible. Congar's call to his Church for a new and "total ecclesiology" that would give the layman his proper place in the Church's life and witness has begun to awaken long-dormant echoes in a Protestantism which had grown content to "leave things to the minister," and which was all too willing to pay for its mimeographed directives to be sent out from the central agencies of the denominations. We must be grateful for the fact that, in its concern for evangelism and for the nature of the Church, the World Council of Churches was ready to explore the new insights and has steadily thrown its weight against the entrenched positions of ecclesiasticism and conservative clericalism.

However, it is time to ask what are the results in terms of the actual involvement of laymen in the evangelical and social witness of the Church. There has been a good deal of talk on these themes for some years, and evangelical academies in the meantime have graduated from the cellars and derequisitioned army hostels to impressive modern buildings with shiny new equipment. But to what extent have they managed to bring the workers of Europe nearer to Jesus Christ? Have they become simply another form of the comfortable "club" in which people who share the same conservative or sentimental radicalism second each other's "advanced" motions about the Church? The "cozy club" has always been the devil's favorite trick for nullifying the witness of the Church, and only those who are engaged in this work can answer these questions. Thank God there are signs that they are not unaware of them.

But the question remains, what are laymen *doing* with the new insights? Have they simply assumed a new *status* in the Church? It is perhaps worth noting the attitude of the administrators in the denominations to a movement like this—attitudes that are always carefully dressed in impeccable theology, but which, underneath, are invariably realistic. An initial hesitation on the part of the more ecclesiastical hierarchies was to be expected, for there was always the fear that the difficult and embarrassing question of orders might be broached, but on the whole we can see that they have welcomed the new accent on the laity. Indeed, they have realized that when it could be combined with a firm emphasis upon stewardship and a policy of inviting representative laymen (especially leading business executives) into the councils of the denomination, the result might be pure gain: no one can understand the mind and methods of the professional ecclesiastical administrator better than a good business executive!

Please do not mistake me—a good deal of this *is* pure gain. The recognition of the place of the layman in the Church will remain one of the most significant contributions of the Ecumenical Movement to the life and thought of the Church within the last generation, but every Christian should be concerned lest this should become simply justification for a new *status*, rather than the call to commitment and witness.

The relation of this to our subject is in the fact that— rightly or wrongly—*the layman's new assurance has been gained at the expense of the parish minister.* To many young people there seems to be less and less justification for the distinctiveness of the pastoral office, and therefore less incentive for a young man to become committed to it. If we are talking about the *total*

ministry of the Church, then the time has come for a fresh examination of the ordained minister in that total ministry. Sooner
or later the theologians of the Reformation traditions will have
to face the question whether ordination means anything at all
in their theology, and if so, what?

Some years ago that extremely perceptive Congregational
layman, B. L. Manning, gave a "charge to the Church" at an
ordination in which he declared, "The sacred ministry of the
Church of God is not a secretaryship, a sort of general manager's job, a device to save trouble for the majority of the
Church members by concentrating nearly all their duties upon
one or two. You cannot ordain a minister as you appoint a
professional at a golf club or an errand boy in a shop. In one
way it is true that our brother is to be your minister, but in a
far deeper and more important way he is a minister of the Word
and Sacraments, a minister of the Gospel, a minister of Christ"
(*A Layman in the Ministry* pp. 152 f.). I agree, for who could
disagree? However, we have frankly to recognize that for many
of our young ordinands and ministers the image of the "general
manager" or "company secretary" seems very close to what
their congregations expect of them, not only in terms of the
daily use of time, but much more fundamentally in terms of
their life goals, far nearer than the "image" of a servant of the
Cross.

If there is a deep spiritual malaise among the young at this
point it centers in the uncertainty that many theological students have about what their real function should be as an
ordained minister. My plea is emphatically not that the Ecumenical Movement should go back on its insights about the
ministry of the layman, but rather that it should first encourage
the churches to implement those insights by calling upon their
laymen for the commitment of witness; secondly, that it should
extend its questioning to that of the *total* ministry of the
Church, in which the man who is called by Jesus Christ to
minister to his people in Word and Sacrament has his proper
place.

Practical Irrelevance

Since the churches have the responsibility of sending delegates to ecumenical conferences, there are plausible reasons why we should expect a high percentage of administrators to represent them on such occasions. But ecumenical assemblies are tending to become the preserve of the various administrative hierarchies. True, among the delegates we will also find a fair sprinkling of "influential laymen" and theologians (usually in that numerical order), and there are reasons why that should be so.

However, when one looks at the representation not so much from the point of view of the misleading distinction between "ordained" and "unordained," but from that of the more real distinction between those who are primarily responsible for the executive administration of the churches and those who are primarily responsible for its thought and worship, then it looks very different. The chances of a parish minister representing his denomination at a major ecumenical assembly are very slight indeed; and, if he is not minister of a large and "successful" parish, nonexistant.

We must not be too sentimental about this. There would be some truth in the charge that many parish ministers are not equipped to represent their denominations ecumenically. A parish minister may not have the necessary background on specific theological and practical issues, he may have been too concerned with local parishes to take the comprehensive view, and he does not exert as much denominational influence as the ecclesiastical administrator, even as the prominent ecclesiastical layman.

Consider the ecumenical experience of the average minister. As a university or seminary student he may have had some opportunity for reaching across the denominational lines, but unless he has been active in intercollegiate or interseminary work (in which case, if he has any ability, he will almost certainly be drawn off into some kind of secretaryship, and will probably

not go near a parish), it is not likely that his ecumenical relationships will be strong enough or vivid enough to flourish and
grow within the boundaries of a normal parish. He will sink into
the groove of working, thinking, and praying for his own congregation, and if he lifts his sights much further it will almost
inevitably be to the missionary work of his own denomination
or to the social needs of the area where he lives. The pressure of
denominational machinery will be upon him to produce its quotas
of "this and that," and the way to "success" in his church lies
through them.

Ironically enough, for most men that is also the only road
open to them for real ecumenical encounter, for if once one of
them can win his place in the hierarchy, he will probably have
the chance of representing his denomination in ever more rarified
and distant orbits of ecumenical encounter. (Incidentally, one
can note that the genuine ecumenical concern of many church
leaders has been born, or at least stimulated, through their
ecumenical contacts at conferences, committees, and assemblies.
One does not begrudge them this; we only covet it for a much
wider circle of ministers.) However, the majority of parish
ministers never "arrive," and therefore the parish minister has
little chance to enjoy ecumenical encounter at anything beyond
the local level—with men who are to some extent "rivals," and
who have all the same cares, preoccupations, and frustrations
as his own.

The tragedy is that it is at this local level that the Ecumenical Movement is most bedeviled by old prejudices and traditional
rivalries, and this is the situation where parish ministers hold
the key positions. If ecumenism fails in the parish its success
elsewhere will not count very much, but we are in a never-ending
spiral: the parish minister cannot gain the necessary insights
into the whole ecumenical problem until he has participated in
it, and he will not have the chance of participating in it until
he has gained the insight! Indeed, his chances grow slimmer as
the prizes in the ecumenical race become bigger. So the ecumenical enterprise is in danger of grinding to a halt at the parish

level, because for all practical purposes the parish minister does not think of it as his major concern.

Our question then is this: How can that spiral be broken? That is the question to which we shall have to address our minds increasingly if the great need that Dr. Wand saw is to be realized. I will simply suggest three possible lines for approaching the problem.

1.

Theologically there is the need to examine again the nature of ministry and ordination. We have perhaps been too afraid of this in recent years for fear of raising again the touchy points about Apostolic Succession, but recent writings from the Episcopal side (notably *The Historic Episcopate*) suggest that there are numbers of Anglicans who are wrestling with this issue from the new perspectives of biblical theology; there is hope that fresh air may be blown through the old controversies.

Be that as it may, it is our duty to look at the whole concept of *Ministry*—not simply of *the* Ministry—and this has to be brought into focus with the ecumenical and biblical insights about the ministry of the laity. Lest there should be any misunderstanding, let me urge that what is wanted is not a concept of ministry to set over *against* that of the laity (as if they were rival emphases to be defended), but rather, in Fr. Congar's expression, a "total ecclesiology" that will do biblical justice to both. We shall have to look at the ministry of the Church, and the ministry of Jesus Christ; we shall have to ask how the minister within *his* ministry re-presents to the Church the ministry of Jesus Christ; we shall have to look again at the Bible and see that those old but misunderstood themes of election and calling, salvation and vocation, are to be seen not in terms of spiritual prestige and status but in terms of a ministry that was summarized in the Cross. In the Christian Church it is always true, "No Cross, no Crown," but almost unconsciously we drift into the error of claiming in ordination a Crown of honor, with-

out seeing that ordination is ordination to service and to the
Cross.

2.

What about the practical question of parish ministers representing their denominations at ecumenical functions?

I suppose at this point one could enter an impassioned plea
for a 25 or 30 percent representation of parish ministers and
priests at the next assembly of the World Council of Churches,
but it would not be very realistic. Moreover, I believe such claims
undercut the biblical view of the Church which the Ecumenical
Movement is beginning to grasp. Of course, there will always
be protests that certain classifications within the Church are
underrepresented: the claims that the laity should have a 50 percent representation will probably continue, and similar claims
may be made for women or for youth. Presumably, if one is
going to argue in this way, one could put in a claim for a 50
percent representation among the lay representatives for those
who work as tradesmen in shirt sleeves as over against those
who work as executives in a collar and tie; or among the ordained representatives for those who come from rural parishes
over against those who work in city parishes; or among theological teachers for those who teach in the biblical fields over
against those in Systematic Theology or Church History. There
is no end to the analysis and classifying that can go on in the
hope that thereby we become more truly representative of the
churches as they are. The World Council of Churches has
brought it to a fine art.

But does this method ever achieve what it sets out to achieve?
You do not represent a fair sample of the American nation by
bringing together a group of British, Germans, Scandanavians,
Italians, Poles, Negroes, and some native Americans and mixing
them in the proportions in which they occur in the USA. You
might do far better, if accurate representation is the only concern, to take the first fifty Americans you meet.

More fundamentally, does not this method *as a method* carry within it an inherent denial of the Ecumenical Movement's best insights about the nature of the Church? By dividing the Church into its different "strata" of age, sex, status, and so forth, do we not virtually contradict that very *wholeness* we have been seeking to promote? An accent which differentiates between clergy and laity, men and women, adults and youth may be useful in giving a rough-and-ready representation of these special interests, but if we become too preoccupied with the distinctions, the sense of the Church's wholeness in life and witness is bound to be weakened.

I do not mean to suggest by this that the churches are necessarily best served by what seems to be an overpreponderance of ecclesiastical administrators at the World Council's assemblies —quite the reverse; but I am suggesting that the churches need to be represented by their *best* men and women, whether they come from administration, scholarship, secular life, or the parish. For we should remember that the Ecumenical Movement is working toward the time when all the stratifications and distinctions that at present divide people inside and outside the Church must be seen in terms of the Church's *total* ministry— that is, as irrelevant and dangerous in terms of status, lay or clerical, but as only important as they contribute by their variety of insight to the "fullness of Christ."

3.

The last question to which we address ourselves is to ask how the parish minister is to be given the kind of living encounter, without which there can be little real ecumenical education.

In part I believe the way has been shown by Bossey. It is significant that Bossey began as a Lay Training Centre, very directly related to the Academy movement in Europe and to all the postwar trends in lay witness. But within a few years of its opening Bossey found that it had to add to its yearly program ecumenical training courses for ministers, priests, and missionaries, and for theological students. This is where the bottleneck was discovered, for it is not much use training a layman to go back to a parish situation where his minister or priest is ecumenically illiterate: it breeds bitterness and suspicion on the part of the minister and frustration for the erstwhile enthusiast. Furthermore, the ecclesiastical facts of life very soon show that one cannot get through to the laymen in some churches except through the ministry.

A great deal more could be done by denominations and by individual parishes to send some of their ministers to these special courses: there they would enter an ecumenical dimension of thinking, worship, and experience that cannot be easily equaled anywhere else in the world. However, the proportion of parish ministers or district missionaries who find their way to the Ecumenical Institute will inevitably remain relatively small in any given year. We have to reproduce the Bossey experience as far as possible in thousands of different localities for ministers who may never get within a thousand miles of the Château de Bossey. Something can be done by using the newer ecumenical centers that have been springing up in different parts of the world, such as the Ecumenical Institute at Evanston, but these cannot begin to meet the real need.

I believe, however, that ecumenical education and *participation* (which is the key to real education in this field) can be conducted on the scale we need if local incentives and resources are used. The Oberlin Conference used many local groups throughout America, and the next Faith and Order Conference could provide sufficient incentive to get ministers' groups and fraternals meeting together and talking on an even wider scale. But such local groups do need to be given direction and help by those who know what the objectives are and who have some knowledge of the available literature and most recent thinking. We might very well use the experience of the increasing number of graduates of the Graduate School of Ecumenical Studies, who so often return home to kick their heels and wonder how on earth they can use the experience they have gained. We could ask the National Council of Churches for help in planning seminars on live ecumenical issues at our denominational summer schools for ministers. (What would happen if five Episcopalians and five Lutherans were invited to participate in a summer camp for United Church of Christ ministers?) We could also ask the National Council to concentrate the summer visitors from overseas in the situations (and in the numbers) in which they can be most effective—so that they are not isolated objects of polite curiosity, but can make a truly international contribution in the places to which they are sent. And we could set all these things within the context where worship and Bible study are a central part of the local program, and not simply a formal salute to the Almighty before the "real business" begins.

The parish minister is often hungry for the spiritual experience and the theological study that will carry him deep. He has to find it in an encounter with his brother minister "down the road," and they cannot find this unless they find themselves as part of a community that goes beyond suspicion and beyond bonhomie. We do not need bigger and better ecumenical conferences with greater representation for parish ministers, but we need more local groups and ministers' fraternals meeting regularly for deep Bible study and hard theological thinking. If that were engaged in faithfully, these men would not only find their deep prejudices disappearing, but they would soon find the need to express their honest differences, their frustrations, and their common hopes in worship. To meet around God's Word together is to meet in the context where we may be surprised by prayer. And when that begins to happen in the parishes, the main point of the Ecumenical Movement will have been won.

CAN THERE BE AN ECUMENICAL THEOLOGY?

Robert Tobias

Robert Tobias was a member of the staff of Inter-Church Aid of the WCC in Geneva, with special responsibilities for Eastern Europe and Orthodox countries. He first came to Europe to serve with CIMADE in France as a fraternal worker. His present position is Professor of Ecumenical Theology at Christian Theological Seminary in Indianapolis.

*E*CUMENICAL theology" as a word and notion seems destined for widespread use, probably with a variety of meanings as wild as those given to the adjective "ecumenical" over the past twenty years. And if Christians are attracted to something called ecumenical theology, they may ponder as did Archbishop Temple concerning the Church Universal: "I believe in the Holy Catholic Church, and regret that it does not at present exist."

Why the current popularity of "ecumenical theology"? Though not a new term or concept, it is increasingly used in ecumenical circles, frequently without definition or examination.*

* Prof. T. W. Torrance, in an article in the *Scottish Journal of Theology*, Vol. VI, March, 1953, asserted that at the Third World Conference

Is it the general mood of our times—toward centralism and rational order—which demands in theology, not just tolerance or purity, but consensus, syncretism, integration? Or, is it perhaps the popular practice of propounding a theology of every separate thing—a "theology of the laity," "theology of work," "theology of worship," "theology of stewardship"—which has come now to construct a "theology for things ecumenical" also? Parenthetically, the proper examination of these phenomena from theological perspectives has long been needed, but the net result should be the provision of adequate theological *foundations for* appropriate functions, not a theological *justification of* existing concepts and practices. The theology of Augustine, or of Luther, or of Cyprian, yes; but a theology *of* stewardship, *of* religious education, and so forth, no.

One further caution at the outset: "ecumenical theology" in popular parlance can easily come to mean either the composite "theology" of the articulate personalities of the Ecumenical Movement, or it can become a theological apologia for the Movement itself. What we are concerned with here is not a theology of ecumenicity, but with the ecumenicity of theology, not simply with the theological issue between churches, within the faith, but the one between the faith and the total world which is the concern of the *oikoumene.*

---

on Faith and Order at Lund, 1952, "real ecumenical theology had taken the field," without further definition but by context evidently meaning the theological methodology common to a large body of Christendom. Dr. H. H. Wolf, Director of the World Council's Ecumenical Institute, has a lecture exploring the nature and method of an "ecumenical theology." Prof. W. M. Horton, in his *Christian Theology, An Ecumenical Approach,* New York, Harper, 1958, uses the term frequently (pp. xii, 1-3, *passim*) and, to his credit, only after an attempt at precise definition. Prof. K. E. Skydsgaard, in an article in the *Ecumenical Review,* Vol. VI, No. 1, 10, Oct., 1953, asks "what is ecumenical theology?" Prof. Nikos Nissiotis, Associate Director of the Ecumenical Institute, used the expression favorably in his address to the New Delhi Assembly of the World Council of Churches, Nov. 24, 1961. Dr. Visser 't Hooft, General Secretary of the World Council, in his Taylor lectures (*The Pressure of Our Common Calling,* Garden City, Doubleday, 1959) on a theology of the ecumenical movement, avoids the term entirely.

I. Is There Now an Ecumenical Theology?

Ask a theological student today to draw up an "ecumenical theology" in outline form and he will likely turn for his sources to the documents of the World Council. It is assumed that the World Council has presuppositions, and is reaching or will reach conclusions which are "ecumenical" and theologically definitive. "Ecumenical theology" to him is that system of doctrinal conclusions which UNIVAC might cull from the pronouncements of that "ecumenical" body.

What has the World Council itself to say on the matter? Does it intend or hope for any kind of "ecumenical theology"? Does it presuppose that there *ought* to be a commonality of doctrine, of mind, of experience?

Explicitly, the World Council speaks theologically almost entirely in terms of ecclesiology. And here it is characterized by two recurrent ideas: *consensus* and *practicality*.

CONSENSUS. It has been assumed in the World Council and out that a consensus is eventually desirable and possible, even necessary for the Ecumenical Movement to fulfill its calling. This is evident in the Movement's direct pronouncements, in its disclaimers, and its methods. It was assumed at the Edinburg Conference in 1910, and before, that "to draw the churches out of isolation into conference" was to allow for some common leavening toward unanimity. The fear of churches in appointing representatives, and of the representatives themselves, was that representatives might appear to compromise basic convictions of the churches represented. Would not a "common mind" imply lack of integrity in particulars? The "neutrality" disclaimer of the Central Committee (at Toronto, 1950)—"Membership of the World Council of Churches does not imply acceptance of a specific doctrine concerning the nature of church unity . . ."— did not mean that there should be no consensus, but that the churches, themselves, not the World Council, should decide upon it, when, what, and how much. As to whether there should be one Church, consensus was already recorded: "the World Council of Churches can have no neutrality on whether that question is answered or not."

The immediate result was a temporary increase in denominational tensions, the larger results were the fading out of the proverbial tension between American and Continental theology, an interpenetration of competent scholars from all areas, and that the great doctrines of faith were taken for granted. "Ecumenical theology has taken the field." In the preface to one of the latest documents of Faith and Order, *One Lord, One Baptism*, Bishop Oliver Tomkins, now chairman of the Commission, writes that whereas the final results of the study are not yet evident, central agreements are expected.

Faith and Order may correctly deny that it expects a synthesis to come out of comparative studies of present ecclesiological data, but it has not disavowed the likelihood and expectation of an ecumenical consensus, whatever its source or sources. Indeed, its four-point mandate and its St. Andrews (now New Delhi) description of churchly unity, whatever "neutrality" was professed at Toronto, presuppose and present a very considerable consensus already acceptable among the churches.

The General Secretary, in his Report to the Third Assembly, was quite explicit: "The expression which St. Paul uses several times, 'to be of the same mind,' speaks of an incomparably deeper and more substantial unity than we can claim to have at present." And in his Taylor lectures he declared that "if negotiation (as a means to *koinonia*) is ruled out, the common struggle for a common mind is not ruled out." However, the other World Council officers have been quick to warn that a common mind does not necessarily mean doctrinal relativism, or uniformity, or conformity—mistaken notions which have long prevented more radical "free" Protestants from ecumenical engagement.

In one of the documents prepared for the New Delhi Assembly some "fears" were listed which illustrate that both those who presumably fear and those who reassure currently anticipate some kind of consensus:

"—the fear of uniformity in doctrine, in practice, and in ways of worship; the hope that with a wider inheritance there will follow a more inclusive apprehension of the Truth in Christ and that such inclusiveness will be compatible with a fruitful diversity.

"—the fear that through compromise we may sacrifice truth that belongs to essential Christian faith; the hope that we may, by obedience to the Holy Spirit, be led into greater apprehension of truth."

There are some basic points of difference, but the assumptions about a consensus in the Ecumenical Movement are not entirely foreign to the Sobornost of Eastern Orthodoxy or to the Old Catholic doctrine of truth from St. Vincent of Lerins: *quod semper, quod ubique, quod ab omnibus creditum est, hoc est vere proprieque catholicum.* The intent and procedures are not yet, however, the same.

While officers of the World Council would hardly claim that it is the task of the Council to *produce* an ecumenical theology, whether expressed as "central agreement," or as "greater apprehension of truth," or as "common mind," or as "complementarity," it is clear that the Ecumenical Movement is widely expected to produce a consensus which could pass for an "ecumenical" theology.

PRACTICALITY. But is a consensus ecumenical? Under what conditions? Is it theological if ecumenical? A consensus, its forging and declaration, is not to be avoided *eo ipso* as evil, but it holds very considerable potential dangers. This is already illustrated in the present "ecumenical consensus" which in its understanding of theology, is inordinately Western, rationalistic, Thomistic (to this we return later), in its understanding of ecumenical as instrumentalist, pragmatic, this-worldly.

Probably for centuries the favorite Biblical passage for "devotions" at ecumenical gatherings has been John 17:21, "that the world may believe. . . ." Oneness must be practical—

for mission. The Central Committee at Rolle, 1951, gave some official status to this pragmatic kind of understanding: "The word 'ecumenical' is properly used to describe everything that is related to the whole task of the whole Church *to bring the Gospel to the whole world*" (italics mine). Later the Division of Ecumenical Action defined "ecumenical work," and presumably it follows for ecumenical theology, as meaning work "which helps the existing churches in process of renewal to become the One Missionary Church." Is that really ecumenical? Is it theological?

In one of the pioneer essays on the subject, "Toward an Ecumenical Theology,"* Dr. H. H. Wolf, Director of the Ecumenical Institute, describes ecumenical theology as one "which reflects the reality of the Church as a whole, so that it can perform the service with which it has been entrusted." Whatever may be said of the ecclesiology there implied (Is man really to see to the shaping of the Church in terms of its effectiveness?), an ecumenical theology which *a priori has* to be, not responsive, declarative, or definitive, but instrumental, can only *contra facto* be *theo*-logical. Instrumentalism is a proper perspective for God, no doubt; but for a theologian?

Practicality has its appropriate place, even as do goals. Dr. Visser 't Hooft, who has warned that "cooperation" is not enough, and sets practicality in proper context in his New Delhi report: "that together you may with one voice glorify the God and Father of our Lord Jesus Christ," identifying that as the "real goal" of the World Council. But the danger of an "ecumenical theology" focused too largely on ecclesiology is that in the desire to be *ecclesiologically* ecumenical, *ergo* practical, it is in danger of becoming *theologically* unecumenical. See what Israel's "ecumenically-minded" men did to Jeremiah!

In the dialectic between "theological truth" and "churchly unity," fruitful work has been achieved ecumenically. There is indeed an impressive area of consensus here represented. But in the issue between what is *given* by God and what are appropriate

* *Ecumenical Review*, 1955, Vol. XIII, 215.

ecumenical *aims*, much more precise thought needs to be given
theologically. Until that is done it would be difficult to speak of
the present consensus, large as it is, as representing an ecumenical *theology*. Behind these explicit achievements in ecclesiological consensus, however, the World Council has probably
made its greatest contribution to ecumenical theology implicitly,
to wit, in the implicit presuppositions and procedures by which
the Ecumenical Movement lives and operates, which may well
prove to be essential components of seminal ecumenical theology.
To this we return later.

II. What Is Ecumenical Theology?

Before the question, "Can there be an ecumenical theology?"
can be answered, it is necessary to define what is meant by "ecumenical theology." Several have done preliminary essays. Prof.
K. E. Skydsgaard defines ecumenical theology as "dramatized
symbolics"—the systematic consideration of the multiverse lines
of doctrine, thought and subjective viewpoint represented in
the ecumenical movement, continually criticized and judged by
the ultimate authority of the truth of God's Word. Professor
Skydsgaard's emphasis seems to be on a comparative dialogue
between existing confessional systems, although his further
elaboration of the method of ecumenical theology as *in via* adds
a quality which transforms what might otherwise be sterile
comparative or synthetic dogmatics, and suggests that precipi-
tated faith in confessional systems *and* living faith are not unrelated. Dr. H. H. Wolf identifies ecumenical theology as the
dimension which determines all theological study, by "theology"
meaning "the whole, continuous process of critical reflection
which is the task of the Church," and, though secondary, is
necessary to the reality of the Church. Ecumenical theology is
one "which reflects the reality of the Church as a whole, so that
it can be what it is and should be so that it can perform the
service with which it has been entrusted." In further elaboration
Dr. Wolf implies that ecumenical theology is confessional or
particular theology carried on in an "ecumenical perspective";

it is not one of neutrality, but of abandonment of exclusivity. Its characteristic form is dialogue involving comparative mutual theological criticism and exhortation with a view toward consensus. Dr. Wolf seems to end up, and if so, correctly, with no fundamental distinction between theology and ecumenical theology when it is the Church voicing it.

Professor Horton defines ecumenical theology in terms of its basic concern:*

A truly ecumenical theology would be one in which various schools of Catholic and Protestant theology would confront each other systematically, and strive toward an ultimate reconciliation, in view of their common concern to interpret the same Christian faith to "all the world" and "every creature" . . . ecumenical theology is neither *un*confessional nor *anti*confessional, but *inter*confessional.

These pioneers invite followers, and a definitive work in the area is needed. Some of the problems involved in the definition and practice of "ecumenical theology" are already evident in their essays, notable of which is the assumption that the basic data of ecumenical theology consist of confessional dogma, that the company of participants is comprised of contemporary Christendom, that the basic method is still comparative study, that the ultimate objective is unanimity.

Implicit behind all ecumenical theologizing is the assumption of its *universal representativeness*. Although past attempts at an ecumenical consensus have presumed too much upon "historical" data, as though no other were involved, ecumenical theologizing will have to take into account that the whole household of faith stretches from the beginning of history to the end of time, comprising all the saints, martyrs, prophets, priests, laity, all the yet to be born.† Ecumenical theologizing

* *Op. cit.*

† Eastern Orthodoxy, which holds in general to this position of totality of representation, finds itself in a most awkward dilemma and has to restrict its theological articulations to the first eight centuries (Seven Councils) because it has been impossible to have the *whole* church together to speak since. As Father Florovsky has pointed out, this makes "Living Tradition" a contradiction.

must involve also in dialogue the faith, the theologies, of that company of witnesses, positing where and as it can such consensus as is evident and vital, pressing forward from there in continuing dialogue, and periodic consensus-taking to the end of time. It is the act of God which puts us to the dialogue, and the dialogue which sends us back again to the act of God. Ecumenical theology, or preferably theologizing, is indeed then, as I believe Dr. L. A. Zander put it, "where *living* theologies find existential engagement with each other."

How, then, define ecumenical theology? This is a task no individual, no communion, no council can do from any presumed objective standpoint. Ecumenical theology will be defining itself *in via*, which is to say that ecumenical theology can never be precisely defined *in history*. The nature of God's continuing revelation to His pilgrims, the interdependence of traditioning and traditions, the generations yet to become articulate make ecumenical theology an eschatological reality, always becoming, never final, but very real to those whose identity in Christ is with the whole sweep of God's history.

III. The Marks of Ecumenical Theologizing

How is ecumenical theologizing done?

We are not able here to establish ground rules. Those concerned with ecumenical theologizing cannot step outside that process to assess it. Nor could any "ground rules," regardless of how carefully delineated and followed, guarantee a product called theology. Indeed, the opposite may more likely happen: adherence to ground rules intended to *produce* theology will *prevent* precisely that from happening. Still, theology is not indiscriminate daydreaming, nor is ecumenical theology all discourse on all subjects by all people through all time. Something here is distinctively identifiable. We note these marks, "starting points" perhaps, which describe what has been happening and the conditions which seem to have prevailed. When fruitful theologizing takes place again it may be under similar conditions. But fortunately for our spiritual condition the same precise conditions cannot be repeated and therefore the same effects cannot be maneuvered with a "Lo, here" or "Lo, there."

LORDSHIP. This is the first mark of ecumenical theologizing: commitment and obedience of those involved to divine Lordship. All else is ultimately expendable: canon, constitution, creed, council, Scripture. The epistemological question, and the way creed, Scripture, and so forth, are involved, follows immediately, but the prior fact is common acknowledgment that we have been apprehended by Him, are His, and are willing to subject subsequent decisions and interests to His Lordship.

Apart from this kind of obedient commitment in common, "ecumenical" conversation may be very interesting philosophy, perhaps even evangelism if only one part is so committed, but it has a different character from that conversation which consciously depends upon the divine Lord.

VISION. God has not only acted, but something further is expected, for which some earnest is already given. What He has done and what He will do, with whatever rich or "heretical" variations, become the substance for ecumenical theologizing. Without this, the Christian community may engage in catechizing, perhaps proselytizing, not theologizing. But if theology must settle for its "vision" it cannot presume to uncover God— the theologian can nonetheless proclaim as (provisionally) objective reality and therefore with boldness and confidence the "that which I received of the Lord," but also as subjectively received and therefore in humility and expectation to be corrected, fulfilled, redeemed in the future.

OPEN-ENDED. We have not yet "arrived," but are always in the process of arriving. Where we are going is being determined for us. The elements of mystery, of dependence, of confidence in the leading of the Spirit are essential aspects of our pilgrimage. This is surely neither accidental, nor resulting from our human limitation. God's action, which is beyond our knowing, as well as the effect of as-yet-unborn history, makes the future a mystery before us. We cannot therefore absolutize any particular canon or dogma or "scheme of redemption", or historical consensus, nor be at all at ease over what appear to be necessary exclusions—heresies, schismatics, apostates.

REPRESENTATIVE. This is still the nexus of ecumenical theologizing. That ecumenical theologizing must represent the *oikoumene* is clear, but who is and speaks for the *oikoumene?* How representative? Can the theologizing process include any less than every presumed act and disparate voice of the Lord, whether through apostles, saints, martyrs, the traditions, confessions, sects, conscientious heretics, novices in the faith, experts, the "company of angels," the yet unborn? No man or group, in history, can say with finality, "Here is the Absolute Word of the Lord."

Without this quality of inclusiveness, however great its risks, we can surely not seriously consider ourselves engaged in the process in which all things are to be united, things in heaven and things on earth.

To these four marks, Lordship, vision, open-ended, representative, must be added the obvious details of spiritual and intellectual integrity: encounter, not withdrawal or noncommittal "tolerance"; study and understanding of the situation and faith of others, clarification of a common vocabulary, provisional articulations in proclamation, consensus, dated creeds, common witness of felt common faith, patience.

Given these kinds of marks, it is evident that a great danger in ecumenical theologizing is relativism. To our human lot it would indeed seem comforting to have some clear principle of selection, some measure for mystery, some precision of vision, which could not only set us on the way but keep a bright End before us. But formal scholasticism is a worse risk than relativism, and in any case it is in the realm of mystery where lies our relationship to the God who can never be fenced about nor fathomed by human mind. Therefore, where these marks are evident there, I should say, is the exciting business of ecumenical theologizing.

IV. Is the Ecumenical Movement Engaged in Ecumenical Theologizing?

This takes a "yes" and a "no" answer. References which could be quoted are too numerous for inclusion here. The following are illustrative.

WITH REGARD TO LORDSHIP. "The World Council of Churches is either a Christocentric movement or it is nothing at all . . . our task is not to create or to invent, but to respond," declared the General Secretary at New Delhi.

The Faith and Order meeting at Edinburgh in 1937 proclaimed: "We are one in faith in our Lord Jesus Christ, the incarnate Word of God. We are one in allegiance to Him as Head of the Church and as King of Kings and Lord of Lords. We are one in acknowledging that this allegiance takes precedence of any other allegiance that may make claims upon us."

At the formal adoption of the World Council's constitution at Amsterdam in 1948, and in the further explication of its Trinitarian implications at the Evanston Assembly in 1954 the World Council clearly intended a centrally Christological position.*

Faith and Order has intensified its emphasis on our dependence on the *living* Lord, in contradistinction to formal doctrinal agreement: ". . . as we seek to draw closer to Christ we come closer to one another. We need, therefore, to penetrate behind our divisions to a deeper and richer understanding of the mystery of the God-given unity of Christ with His Church. . . . The way to the center is the way to unity."†

Primary commitment is not to a position, nor yet to historic institutions, but to a Lord, and the starting point is common faith in that One Lord. Faith and Order begins therefore not

---

* For a more detailed study of this issue of Christological lordship, see W. M. Horton, *Toward a Reborn Church,* Harper, N.Y., 1949, and the *Work Book and Report* of the Evanston Assembly, 1954.

† *The Third World Conference on Faith and Order,* SCM Press, 1953, p. 15.

with "problems" or principles, but with One who is known and what consequently can be affirmed. In this process of (may the world be permitted?) Christologizing, Faith and Order finds itself again close to Chalcedon; it is yet to be seen whether its attitude of articulation will be more rational and scholastic or evangelical.

While the self-image of the World Council is explicitly that of being under Christ's Lordship, and the constituent churches have formally declared the same, among the member churches are some which equivocate on this crucial matter, and the World Council knows it. How serious, then is the World Council about Christ's Lordship? Is it an instruction of the Lord to include within the *koinonia* those who openly declare another understanding of Christ, or is it a rationale determined by other considerations? And if the latter, whose is the *koinonia*? Is this a question which can wait for resolution or must it not be settled from the start? Presumably it is in the interest of wider "ecumenical" participation that the World Council has sat loosely in the application of Christocentric principle. Has *oikoumene* then been spread larger thereby than by *in Christo*? Is *ecumenical* so broad that it is no longer *theologizing*?

WITH A VISION AND EXPECTATION. A vision received and the expectation of fulfillment in some form have characterized Faith and Order since the first letters of invitation for the Preliminary Conference in Geneva, 1920. While the details have not been spelled out as clear, that there is a "given" and a "becoming," that we should be joined together in the receiving and manifesting of them has been largely unquestioned. Here, though this present study is limited principally to Faith and Order, it should be added that the work of other departments of the World Council have reflected their own "visions" of unity, not without theological foundations, of a world at peace, of racial brotherhood, of economic and social responsibility, and so on, which should not be detached from the expectation of churchly unity.

The boldest articulation of what, in some detail, the One

Church might be expected to look like is set forth by the
Commission on Faith and Order at St. Andrews, in 1960.

We believe that the unity which is both God's will and his gift to
his Church is being made visible as all in each place who are baptized
into Jesus Christ and confess him as Lord and Saviour are brought
by the Holy Spirit into ONE fully committed fellowship, holding the
one apostolic faith, preaching the one Gospel, breaking the one
bread, joining in common prayer, and having a corporate life reaching out in witness and service to all and who at the same time are
united with the whole Christian fellowship in all places and all ages
in such wise that ministry and members are accepted by all, and
that all can act and speak together as occasion requires for the tasks
to which God calls his people.

The problem of vision and expectation in the Ecumenical
Movement is the one ever before God's seers. To be able to
articulate what is "given," though dimly, in sufficiently provisional language as not to displace the reality with the description, and yet sufficiently clearly as to enable it to become
a more manifest reality is the inescapable tension and challenge.
On this point Eastern Orthodoxy may have more to say, indeed
is already saying more to the rest of the Ecumenical Movement
than the rest is able to hear.*

As OPEN-ENDED. What lies behind the vision given, sub-

* Unity among men in the Church is the result, the reflection, of the
event of the Father's Union with Christ by His Spirit realized in the historical Church on the day of Pentecost. . . . Unity is not an *attribute* of the
Church, but it is its very *life*. . . . [It] is not something given to the Church
from a source outside the Church after that Church has arisen from other
causes. It is the *sine qua non* of the very existence of the Church implanted
by the Holy Spirit among men. . . . Thus "unity" does not mean waiting
for agreement to be reached between the different conceptions which are
held in our churches, but imposes on us the obligation to remain in that
condition in which we are re-created by the Spirit as One in the One
Undivided Church. It is not only through consideration of "what" we
believe this Church Unity to be that we hope to advance to the continuous
re-establishment of reunion, but also through "how" we (in context, presumably meaning not ethics, but how we are given to) exist as Christians. . . ."
Dr. N. Nissiotis, Address to the Third Assembly of the World Council,
Nov. 24, 1961.

jectively received, is still of God's creation and beyond man's ken or control. The mysterious quality of divine action has been clearly recognized in ecumenical pronouncements, with the consequent recognition that (1) we do not know the shape of things to come: "We are convinced that our unity of spirit and aim must be embodied in a way that will make it manifest in the world, though we do not yet clearly see what outward form it should take. . . . God has yet more light to break forth from His Holy Word for a humble and waiting Church,"* and therefore we cannot make final claims for our own denominations nor any consensus among them; that (2) it is He, the Holy Spirit, who will guide to all truth, and therefore our dependence on Him;† and that (3) therefore our "search for the true unity (John 17:23) . . . must continue until the end of time. Even if all churches in the world would unite today and have a common faith and order, this goal would still be before them. For that ultimate unity in which Christ is all in all is eschatological and belongs in its fullness to the wholly new life of the kingdom."‡

I cite two of the leading contemporary ecumenical statesmen, both Orthodox, as illustrative. Prof. Hamilcar Alivisatos of the Greek Church, in discussing relations between Orthodoxy and Protestantism, wrote: "Certain theological discussions and conferences . . . have shown that, in spite of the existing difficulties, there is still very much common ground. Why then may we not believe that the Holy Spirit will lead to some *unexpected solution?* [italics mine]. We all believe in the one Pentecost, why should we not expect in a second one to come which will be more glorious because it will prove that 'that which is impossible with man is possible with God.' "§

---

* *Second World Conference on Faith and Order*, L. Hodgson, Macmillan, N.Y., 1938, p. 254; Third World Conference, Lund, London, SCM Press, 1953, p. 24.

† Hodgson, *op. cit.*, p. 239.

‡ Visser 't Hooft, *op. cit.*, p. 85.

§ "The Proposed Ecumenical Council and Reunion" *Ecumenical Review*, Oct., 1959, Vol. XII, No. 1, p. 10.

And Prof. Georges Florovsky, in an article describing the ethos of the Orthodox Church, wrote:

Tradition in the Church is not merely continuity of human memory, or the permanence of rite and habits. Ultimately, "tradition" is the continuity of divine assistance, the abiding presence of the Holy Spirit. The Church is not bound by "the letter." She is constantly moved forth by "the spirit." The same Spirit, the Spirit of Truth, which "spake through the Prophets," which guided the Apostles, which illumined the Evangelists, is still abiding in the Church, and guides her into the fuller understanding of the divine truth, from glory to glory.*

Now, Prof. Florovsky cannot believe that, unless he *makes room* for the Holy Spirit to guide, which means no closure, but also continual review—*Living* Tradition. Further along he adds that

since our different "blocs" of insights and convictions did actually grow out of a common ground and were in fact products of a *disintegration* of the Christian mind . . . the very problem of Christian reconciliation is not that of a *correlation* of parallel traditions, but precisely that of the *reintegration* of a distorted tradition.†

Where is the common base for reintegration, assuming that no one has absolutized an existing "base"? This is the unresolved problem in ecumenical conversation. When we push past the authoritative claims of *sola Scriptura*, and consensus, and traditions, by what common epistemology is truth discerned? The open-endedness of present ecumenical conversation is not without reservation—particularly by those who presume to have settled the epistemological question—but it seems to have moved beyond the pitfalls of ultimate relativism and brittle dogmatism. Whether another epistemology, perhaps of "wholity," will ensue is yet to be seen—and bears explicit and careful consideration.

In Representativeness. Here is the Charybdis and Scylla of the Ecumenical Movement. How representative? Representa-

* *Ecumenical Review*, Jan., 1960, Vol. II, No. 2, p. 187.
† *Ibid.*, p. 197.

tive of what, or whom? Of the transcendent Word alone? Of contemporary denomiations? Of all God's people through all time? Which of His people in which time? Anglicans, Lutherans, Old Catholics, Orthodox, Presbyterians, yes. But Monophysites, Pentecostals, Southern Baptists? Is it even conceivable that one *koinonia* and process can comprehend the "Protestant principle" with its emphasis on individual response and "democratic" gradulism, the *Corpus Juris Canonici* with its spirit of finality and centralistic procedure, the Holy Tradition with its infinite "wholeness" and historic doxophany, and conservative Biblicism with its unquestioned authority and proselytizing fervor? Are there limits, within the Christian faith, as to who may participate in ecumenical theologizing?

The Christological clause in the World Council's statement of "basis" is apparently intended as a safeguard of "purity" on one crucial point. Yet to this have now (at New Delhi) been added two other provisos: "according to Scripture," and "do make manifest." This is not the place to discuss *whether* the direct line of communication from the transcendent Word can be safeguarded, but if it were to be, how much or how little would safeguard it? Which doctrines? The problem of Augustine and Meldinius is still with us: "In essentials unity, in nonessentials liberty, in all things charity." What is essential to purity? Purity is apparently controlled from the other end. Can man do more by way of guarantees than to receive Him and articulate that in community?

Or, if representativeness is to be determined on the principle of "wholity," that still presupposes a measure of discrimination. In ecumenical theologizing, at one stage, none who is conscientiously concerned can be excluded who manifests the marks set forth above. And is this not in fact what the World Council has done? The practical and statistical half of its criterion for membership—how large? how autonomous? how regarded by neighbor churches and confessional body?—has not prevented the World Council from involving Pentecostals, Roman Catholics, Southern Baptists, and other Christians whose churches could not presently qualify for membership from its theologizing processes. The practice of the World Council would appear to be preferable to the "letter": the World Council is not simply "neutral" on doctrinal conclusions (Toronto), positions *are* provisionally stated. It is concerned for "purity" Truth, but recognizes its own historic limitations in apprehending it. The complexities here involved, stemming from the Ecumenical Movement's body-spirit nature, need further exploration in hopes of clarification. In the meantime, two or three points should be noted, perhaps by way of caution, under the heading, "representativeness."

In its present, somewhat indeterminate, stance in this matter, a too strong and undefined emphasis on "neutralism" will not result in that at all. At this stage neutralism will mean "drift"—whether deliberate or not—by virtue of the fact that some are more articulate (or less genteel) than others in stating a position and getting a following, or even the simple fact that some languages are more used than others. "Neutrality" combined with "majority" must be scrupulously watched lest the important "still small voice" not be heard.

The Ecumenical Movement seems presently to move in the direction of "wholity," in terms both of constituency and concept. And as it consciously questions both dogmatic fixations and neutralism, the World Council is likely to be tempted toward some kind of comprehensive syncretism or relativism. It may be hoped that the understanding of wholity which is coming will be determined more by the Council's Eastern constituency than its Western, because the kind of "purity" which ought to be involved is more likely derived from that understanding than the Western. *Thereafter* one might then expect to find discussions of consensus less in the setting of ecclesiastical order, of academic discipline, rational speculation and legal obligation, less a concern for consensus of individuals in a historic situation, and more in the setting and consensus of the totality of the Holy Church through all time. In any case it is clear that for the Ecumenical Movement, concern for "purity" and for wholeness, like spirit and body, are inextricably related, and that the present constitution and pronouncements are not final.

IN CONDUCT OF DIALOGUE. So far as the simple ground rules of dialogue are concerned, the fact that the conversation among theologians of diverse traditions is at once more energetic, straightforward, and amicable than that within many of the member denominations speaks for itself. And where there have been instances of less forthrightness and integrity than might have been expected, this has represented hardly more than one missed beat in the total symphony. The limitations most acutely felt have to do with lack of time, and lack of language. Ecumenical theologizing depends upon both.

SHADOWS AND LIGHT AHEAD. Finally, some likely problems which the Ecumenical Movement will face in its theologizing should at least be noted.

1. Juristic responsibility versus sensivity to the Spirit. In its far-flung endeavors on behalf of refugees, famine victims, missions, international affairs, youth work camps, and so on, the World Council has had of necessity to become a legal entity and take responsible—official—decisions. How far will the mood of legal responsibility, "all decisions must be official," affect the spiritual sensitivity and prophetic voice of the Movement? Many have become very concerned by the apparent trend at New Delhi away from charismatic leadership toward official representativeness.

2. The whole Movement versus the sum of its parts. Various documents state or imply that the World Council can do or say no more than the will of the member churches. At the same time it has been recognized that the World Council, under the Spirit, is more than the sum total of its parts. In this dilemma, have the member churches the courage to recognize that this "new entity" may be called to speak another word than they, receive that word, and sustain it? If not, ecumenical theologizing can be done by a computing machine.

3. Neutralism and heresy. The Ecumenical Movement is committed to waiting for general consensus to determine ideo-

logical position. If, as Professor Horton suggests, the function of ecumenical consensus is to "exclude destructive extremes and define a general area of agreement, within which many rival theories may co-exist," the Movement, like ancient Israel, will need to be careful not just to dismiss unpleasant persons or ideas by regarding them as "destructive extremes." A "loyal opposition," for the moment, may be a very healthy thing.

4. Ecumenical ecclesiology versus ecumenical theologizing. Dr. Visser 't Hooft indicates that we do not yet have a theology of the ecumenical movement, but may be doing some ecumenical theologizing. One might be more deeply concerned if the Council *does* achieve a "theology of the ecumenical movement" and quits ecumenical theologizing. The theologizing of the Ecumenical Movement, in its concern for ecclesiology and *church* union, "the nature of the relation within the churches," must also comprehend Life and Work—the cosmos—and not as detached "theologies."

5. Personal experience and objective system. The wisdom of modern man has cast suspicion upon "personal experience" in religion. If St. Paul, so oft quoted in some parts in ecumenical dialogue, were to appear before an ecumenical gathering today with his Damascus road story, there would likely be some embarrassment. While recognizing the problem and possibiilty of unbridled extremes, must not *theo*-logical circles make larger place for this "foolishness to men?"

Can there be an ecumenical theology? Presumably there can, but in terms of a whole system, not until the end of the age. In the meantime, the whole people of God are, consciously or unconsciously, incorporated in a trans-historical community which is the theologizing. If alive spiritually at all, they are engaged in ecumenical theologizing. Are they equipped for it? Under God, this is the task of the Ecumenical Movement.

OIKUMENE *AND THE MILKMAN?*

John Garrett

> *John Garrett* served several years as Director of the WCC's Information Department and Editor of the Ecumenical Press Service, following previous service as General Secretary of the Australian Council of Churches. At present he is Warden of Camden Congregational Theological College in Sydney.

*A*T the end of an important ecumenical meeting held in a European country a group of journalists stood about, dismantling microphones and deciphering their shorthand. They had been let in on the mysteries of "rapid social change" and "responsible emancipation." For an hour the vocabulary of the "Geneva in-group" had crackled in their astonished ears. They were impressed by it all: high level stuff. One of them, a correspondent of an international wire agency, tickled his ear with a pencil and ran his fingers through his hair before going off to file his message. "I'm wondering," he said, "what all this is going to mean to the Kansas City milkman."

It is never easy to persuade professional or semiprofessional ecumenists that the milkman matters. Most of them come from one of two social groups: academics and administrators. Each group is custodian of a private world. Each private world seems eminently desirable to its inhabitants, who have had to carve niches for themselves by dedicated ambition and a tussle for status. Professors of the liberal arts variety are inwardly condescending to those who are not familiar with the mysteries they interpret to selected audiences. Theological professors share in the liberal arts outlook. As one of them, still young, said to me as I struggled with a recalcitrant flashbulb among the public lions of the Faith and Order enclave: "What a vulgar business."

He was right. Communication is always vulgar when it goes beyond a certain distance. Hands become dirty and cherished "concepts" and "notions" lose their precisions in the welter of simplified images that must dilute, soil, and exasperate. In a mass culture of promiscuous communication it is distressing for the scribes to see their precious handiwork subjected to all the risks that were taken in the Incarnation.

Listen to learned arguments in World Council of Churches circles concerning the niceties of communication. Only that which is fully personal is believed to communicate. There must be a meeting of minds. All else is manipulation. The possibility of dialogue must exist. Monologue disrupts the I-thou relationship. The mass media by their nature deface and distort. Words like "journalist" and "popular" produce a shock of negative emotion.

Many of the people who hold and voice these opinions believe in preaching, or precut sacramental worship forms, or both. Once they have evolved their own views of the nature of authority, they become unapologetic authoritarians. They do not welcome dialogue in the form of active and jocular lay criticism. When they are asked to answer sets of short questions on television they are often plunged into a state of acute anxiety about their public image; their answers are frequently opaque and inept. They have no clear conception of the language or thought patterns of those likely to be watching them at any given hour of the day. At least some invisible, and fortunately to them imperceptible, "dialogue" then takes place; their viewers are mercifully provided with facilities to switch

to another channel. Television viewing can be selective, as suffering under sermons cannot. Television is intensely personal.
One human being communicates, for good or evil, with one
other, and at close range. The I-thou relationship is effectively
established. "I see thee," says the viewer. "I do not like thee.
I dispense with thee." Church viewer ratings on many television
programs with an "ecumenical" tinge tend, on the whole, to
prove this point.

What is true for the theology professor is not true for the
administrator. In many countries the professional virtuoso behind the big church desk tends to bask and purr when the
kleig lights are turned on. He acquires a taste for "public relations," dresses consciously for camera effect, actively cultivates
a hearty style with reporters and is able to sit apart to "fill in
off the record" for those who are already *persona grata*. He
covets space in *Time, Life, Newsweek,* even *Paris Match* and
Der Spiegel. If he has gained the knack he can do well for himself and his organization, like any adept foreign ministers with
front men to usher them in to press conferences "on the hour."
The World Council of Churches, since its Evanston Assembly,
has been able to wash, shine, and present itself through its
various spokesmen in this way.

If, in some countries at least, church administrators are
able to handle such occasions with aplomb, then what is wrong
with them? What private world do they endeavor to protect?
In the ecumenical scene it is a world of inevitable institutional
self-justification. We need not deplore this. The laws of institutions drive their architects and custodians to take pride in
what they serve. But suppose, for the sake of argument, that
in the World Council of Churches a large sum of money should
be spent in making a wrong appointment for a welfare project
in a key Asian city. Does the Ecumenical Press Service follow
its criterion of objectivity by giving the human and financial
details? Surely that would be a story the larger church public
and the wider world should know, if only that the mistakes
should not be repeated. On such questions, the Ecumenical

Press Service, which is an objective publication serving a number of ecumenical bodies, observes discreet silence. For all its objectivity it lacks balance at such points, and not always for ethical reasons. I speak as an ex-editor with an uneasy conscience about omissions and paraphrases I made to protect an institution I admire.

In editing the Press Service, or determining the headlines and leads for occasional news bulletins, the role of the administrator becomes confused and difficult. The Hungarian Uprising of 1956 offers an instance. If the whole truth were told about the participation of church members in the Uprising and its suppression, there would be blushes on all sides and many people on each side of the embattled forces would be involved in explanations, denials, and probably house arrest or worse. Yet all journalists with a sense of responsibility to other human beings will occasionally suppress names or details in the interest of saving life or preventing unnecessary suffering. The line between this responsible action and the path of institutional whitewashing is irritatingly fine. The church administrator, without being aware of it, often pleads responsibility when he is indulging in suppression of vital but uncomfortable truth. He naturally identifies public interest with the interest of his limited official concern. Is it in the general interest to make known the details of speeches delivered in the Greek parliament about the private lives of the clergy? Such items are not mere scurrilous titbits. They are essential for a connected view of church-state relations and clergy-laity relations in contemporary Greece. If they were to be inserted in the Ecumenical Press Service, a tedious correspondence with the leaders of the Church of Greece would be inevitable. The staff of the World Council of Churches is too busy to become involved in such time-wasting correspondence, followed by journeys and official explanations. The best that can be done is to encourage good journalists to "write the stories for themselves," by patient interviewing and research on the spot. Yet if it is known that some staff member of the World Council actively encouraged the presentation of this better balanced picture, there would be diplomatic regrets and explanations.

What solution is offered for the dilemma posed by these tensions? It might be objected by a sophisticated observer that all this is known already, that it is inevitable once an organism becomes an organization with central nervous and skeletal systems, it then develops signs of arthritis. There is certainly some law like this implicit in the development; but all depends on the type of staff engaged and how the staff is trained. In the world of the ecclesiastical administrator people are assigned "desks" and carry "portfolios." They indulge in weighty and confidential interoffice memoranda. They distribute copies of their correspondence lavishly over several countries. They are remote from the mud and jungle of East Bengal, the flies and heat haze of Central Australia, the coughing of the tubercular in the shanty towns of Peru. To be sure, they can sometimes write in a polished way about the needs of all these places; but they do not communicate effectively with the people of the places when they go to them on flying visits, or not for the most part. They have a language of their own, a style of life of their own. They really believe that their "consultations" of "leaders and experts from over fifty countries" are more important than the misery of some lonely suburban clergyman preaching to a dwindling set of old-age pensioners in an industrialized area where the churches have failed to understand the change. They might say in principle that they exist for such a man, that they do not consider themselves of more importance than his crisis. But in fact they do!

Perhaps the time has come for the World Council of Churches to write into its staffing policy its early practice of short-term staff appointments, for people who are pioneers by inclination and nonconformists by temperament. A good test is the ability of the person being hired to "live rough" in any part of the world for some weeks and at short notice. There comes an ominous preference among staff for hotel rooms with private baths and stenographers in the retinue at conferences.

There are aggrieved silences in the face of remarks that cut through the woolly verbiage to the real truth of official reports. I was talking one day to a seasoned missionary who had seen long, hard service in two fields. He told me about one of my staff colleagues who visited him in the rambling tropical house where he spent his second term. The house smelt bad. In the morning my colleague had arrived at breakfast with his wrinkled nose buried in a large handkerchief. "Aren't your drains out of order?" he inquired. The missionary said "we have no drains."

The bearing of this on communication may not seem obvious. I am making the point that the routine stamp of administrator is bad for communication in both directions. He alienates the man in the field because he treats his own concerns as normative and central. He destroys effective communication *from* the field by requiring the field man to speak his language and approximate his behavior. This, in fact, is what has happened, in my opinion, in recent years, within the staff of the Youth Department of the World Council of Churches. In this milieu, to use the space age terms, some words are "go" and others "no go." The Youth Department used to have the beginnings of a popular illustrated magazine. They killed it in favor of what they now call a "think piece." This is supposed to circulate among "key youth leaders."

Picture a key youth leader on his home front. He comes home late on Saturday night from wandering between this group and that at his teen-age Rock Session in the old church hall. He has talked to three or four congenial kids about not going too steady just yet. He led the prayers and talked about God's love. When they heard the word "love" they whistled. He has a communication problem on his hands. The key youth leader slumps into his study chair and starts to turn up Bible passages for Sunday morning. His eye falls on the handsome false cover of the WCC's economy offset document collection, not called *Youth*. It is the "think piece." He looks at the table of contents. It says: "Introduction: to the Problem and the Bulletin" (the problem is "living ethics"). He reads a bit of it. It goes on about "problems which are, or ought to be, urgent for youth workers throughout the *oikoumene*" (presumably, he muses, knowing Greek, "the whole inhabited universe"). So onward he goes to "Holy Living in the Modern World." Will this be about Jeremy Taylor, a kind of rehash? No. It is about "involvement" and "commitment." The language is Youth Department "go" language; one could knock a study circle cold with it at a World Student Christian Federation Study Conference. On he goes further: it looks in places more hopeful; but no; here we have "Political Ethics After Niebuhr and After Troika." His final reply to the question posed at the tail end of the "think piece" is negative. It asks him "Can we promise Ethical Growth?" He thinks perhaps not. He goes back to his Bible.

This local youth worker has no desire to be either a professor or a church administrator for life. He is interested in the kids on that dance floor. But the people who are drawn off the dance floor, or out of the local leader's study, into the ecumenical youth circus find that to be "go" in there they must conform. They must speak the language of the "think piece." Sooner or later they too, if they are lucky, will have a "desk," be noticed by theological faculties as "coming men," gravitate into the circles where ecumenists communicate with ecumenists. These remarks are not designed as cruel fantasy. They are based on fact.

Communications means more than information. In the end, as Visser 't Hooft, the World Council of Churches' General Secretary has frequently pointed out, it implies long-range educational processes. These in turn, to work, must be carried through by people who can identify. Good schoolteachers invent a language that is eloquent in the terms already apprehensible within their classes. They explain, imagine, struggle over terms that ignite the spark of recognition and illuminate unfamiliar facts and ideas. Philippe Maury, the present director of the World Council's information work, is keenly interested in introducing prepared curriculum materials into the elaborately

organized Christian education programs of many of the Council's member churches. To undertake this effectively he and his
colleagues will need more than the goodwill and cooperation
of the Youth Department. The youth secretaries are supposed
to be able to communicate to the group that lies roughly between
the ages of sixteen and thirty-five. In fact, as has been indi-
cated, they are often not communicating. They are simply
skimming over the surface and attracting people with their own
inclinations, training, and vocabularly, in much the same way as
a magnet might pull a few steel filings out of an otherwise
unresponsive mixture.

To communicate through education the World Council of
Churches needs, and has cultivated, not without trouble, the
formidable forces represented in the World Council of Christian Education. This body, broadly speaking, inherits the
rather antiquated structures of the Sunday school movement
of the last century. It has, in spasms, absorbed the successive
influences of John Dewey's "learning through doing" and the
more recent craze for "group dynamics." Through its influence
on the shape of curricula, its potential is very great; but since
it embraces a financial interest within the churches and covers
the whole range of intracongregational teaching, from cradle to
grave, it has in the past been jealous of its prerogatives among
youth. Not without justification, it has resented the thought
that the quaint intellectual language—"ecumense"—of the
World Christian Youth Conferences, might start to compete
with the simple real life stories and uncomplicated Bible studies
of the curriculum materials now produced in most countries by
thousands and millions of copies.

The problem in relations with the World Council of Christian Education does not arise at exactly this point. If the
WCCE can succeed in wheedling the WCC's Youth Department
out of the ivory tower and into the vegetable patch, that will
be a glorious work. In the WCCE the difficulty is institutional
rather than one of method and aim. It could be called the
"youth director complex" and consists in that odd insecurity

that overtakes many professional Christian educators at about
age forty. Between twenty-five and forty, life for these administrators, group workers, conference organizers and teachers of
teachers is full and rewarding. At forty many ask the question:
"What do I do next?" They are too old to be sportive among the
young. They find themselves shot at by theologically better
versed people of the same age. The upper echelons of the administrations of their own churches and of ecumenical bodies tend to
be filled by virtuosi rather than pedagogues. They therefore
try to stay on and cling to what they have. Their ways are
already set. They do not respond readily to new ideas or new
ways of doing things. As they look at the flexibility and budgets
of government-sponsored general education they suffer from
inferiority feelings. How does one compete with educational, or
noneducational television in the shaping of the child mind?
They are not trained in the mass media. Even their radio for-
mats and publication layouts lag far behind the equivalents for
secular mass publics, with their advertising revenue, flair, and
just-sufficiently-avant-garde design policies. The "youth directors" and "Christian education directors" are often fine people;
but they are regarded in much the same way as pilots of DC3's
who land and take off on the same runway as Boeing 707's; and
they feel like it.

Their malaise helps to explain why the harnessing of visual,
practical, and planning resources for the ecumenical movement
is slow hard work. The material lies ready to hand in the accumulated insights of ecumenical meetings from Edinburgh, 1910, to
Delhi, 1961. Much of what has been written in the reports of
the meetings is potentially revolutionary, but only potentially.
The ecumenical movement has its John R. Motts, March Boeg-
ners, William Temples, and Eivind Berggravs. In their own
way they are universal men. But the movement awaits its basic
educator; a person of vision who is equally at home in the conference room, the village, the suburb and the factory; who has
the ability to unite theological awareness with educational planning, a sense of the mass media, a wary eye toward bureaucracy

and a preference for pictures and actions. (A perceptive collector of the dreary draft documents at a World Council of Churches Assembly once said: "In the ecumenical movement of the twentieth century the Word was made paper.") This hypothetical "ecumenical Gandhi" might well be a future general secretary of the World Council of Christian Education, with a mandate to rework everything from top to bottom; to dream up a new shape for Christian Education policy. The sequel would be a stream of pictures, books, charts, films, broadcasts, all designed to bring the dammed-up catchment of modern ecumenical discovery to Christians and non-Christians all over the world. It is all there, but the big dam is a hopeless investment without networks of power lines, and irrigation channels into the remotest corners of the parched towns and villages lower down, which, after all, provided the workers for the dam.

If it is to communicate, the ecumenical movement now enters the stage where it sees it must go further than conceiving of its task as regular festivals and pilgrimages for the academic-administrative elites. Theoretically this has been the aim of the study of Rapid Social Change and of the preparatory study for the New Delhi Assembly in 1961. In each of these two cases, local experience proves that we lack the people to bring the issues alive in the local community. In preparing the text of the study book for New Delhi the "in-group" made a genuine, but pathetic attempt to "pitch it simple"; pathetic because they failed miserably when they were sure they were succeeding. Examine the groups that did the writing: you will find they are for the most part composed of "the same old experts," whose manifold talents do not include standing in an exposed place at short notice and saying what they mean in words of one syllable. The baffled sadness of reasonably intelligent laity at the local level, at least in my country, had to be seen to be believed, when they tried to read the theme documents and Bible studies after looking at all the wonderful photographs.

The educational process is bound up with the use of the mass media. It becomes painful to communicate in those parts of the

world where newspapers, magazines, film, radio, and television
shape whole cultures. Advertising and publicity have created a
new vernacular. There is no way out for us, beyond learning
and speaking it. Theologians, purists, guardians of *langues
exquises* detest journalese. Yet it is in the substratum of journalese and the jingles of the radio commercials that a crisp new
koine is being born. The Gospel must be presented in hard-cut
gems rescued from this rough cut ore.

Helping the development is a thankless job for the World
Council of Churches, even if its committees and staff see the
point; mostly they don't. There are many reasons standing in
the way. The Council has been mean from the beginning in its
budgeting for interpretation. Only after six years of temporiz-
ing was there any coordinated policy in relation to daily or
church press. Publications of the various departments were at
that time without benefit of real design. They even made
stodgier reading than they do today. The information budget,
by comparison with expenditure in other international bodies, is
proportionately ludicrous in relation to the importance of the
task. A better coordinated publications policy has up to the
present born little fruit, simply because it is almost impossible
to register the thought that good publications, to be effective,
must be translated by exceptionally able people into the official
languages, and then, more important, promoted by trained
and gifted executives, at high cost, which yields returns after
some years in roughly geometrical progression based on the out-
lay. This simple lesson of all modern mass communication has
not yet penetrated the Council's top planning bodies. They are
still so busy inquiring in depth into the theological and sociological rationales of this or that venture for the future, that
they feel they must conserve funds, which might be otherwise
earmarked for rendering intelligible and accessible all the ad-
mirable "studies in depth" that are lying round already in their
pigeonholes. A fully financed and well staffed office of publications and promotion seems to be a top priority. Working with
the Information and all other departments, it would have to

spend much of its time and talent in the insulting, but necessary task of turning departmental jargon into proper equivalents —in other words rewriting, and teaching people who cannot write for a wide public to do so.

The radio and television industries offer an open field for communication of the ecumenical idea. Here again budget is needed. Up to now the World Committee for Christian Broadcasting, a body with some good ideas but no money, has kept a discreet distance from the World Council of Churches. The relationship may be described as friendly, but not with a view to marriage. Pentecostal and Faith groups, along with the Roman Catholic broadcasters, are cultivated by the WCCB. They believe they might lose these "busy big brothers" from their fellowship if they come too close to the suspect "machine" of the WCC. Now is the time, in my opinion, for the work of the WCCB to be merged in the concerns of the World Council of Churches for effective Christian action in the fields of radio and television. A new staff member, recently appointed, will watch over such a prospect. The moment is opportune because of the integration of the World Council of Churches with the International Missionary Council.

It was a commonplace among people interested in the vast and complicated world of mass communications that the committees and staff of the IMC were babes unborn there. Apart from the excellent, but strictly specialist, *International Review of Missions*, the IMC throughout its history ran little more than doctored up "publicity" folders and "missiological monographs." The *World Christian Books* series, toward the end of its separate existence, broke for a while, on a limited circulation basis, into the publishing business, but when newspaper reporters came on the scene the tendency was to clutch one's papers, turn, and run in the other direction. The trend was to insist that the work of the IMC was essentially "high level" and "of a confidential nature." When the antimissionary nationalist movements in the emerging continents became a news story, when the IMC was accused, by faith missions, of somehow influencing colonial gov-

ernments in the direction of "shutting out the sects," when
strife broke out within the IMC over the advisability of being
swallowed in the WCC whale, some proper arrangements had
to be made to receive the curious knots of journalists who hung
about waiting for the truth. Yet, broadly, the response to such
pressures, was late, reluctant, and practically unbudgeted.

Now that the two world bodies are one, the time has come
for proper expenditure within the new Division of World Mission and Evangelism, on public interpretation of the "crisis and
metamorphosis" of missionary activity outside the Western
world. The need is the more urgent because so many mission
boards are raising funds on false pretenses. It is still assumed in
many "sending" countries, that the Western missionary is a
source of cultural light, life, and civilization, and will sooner
or later be appreciated as such among the recipients of the ex-
port. This gratuitous falsehood is in many places being coun-
tered, not least through the fine work done across the years by
the IMC; but the old false image must be dispelled by proper
press relations and by the imaginative use of television, in particular, as it arrives in the world's new nations.

The American churches alone have so far seen the possible
bearing of radio and television as a cultural "presence" on the
entire future of their work abroad. They alone have done at
least something on a large scale to establish transmitters and
train nationals to use them creatively, and not only for "religious" programs. The coordination of this work has taken place
largely thrugh the Mass Communications staff of the missionary
part of the National Council of Churches in the USA.

If the American mission boards were to insist that a trained
international staff should now be appointed by the WCC, to
serve the whole Council in the interpretation of the world mission of the Church, the influence of their combined secretaries
and executives might be sufficient to coordinate and consolidate,
with a far better budget, the combined work of the World Committee for Christian Broacasting, the American churches, the
WCC's Information Department, and the various missionary

literature agencies and magazine enterprises. From a focus created in this way technical and spiritual advice and aid could flow to nationals at work in all parts of the world: ideas, photographic resources, films and film clips, sound recordings, could all be beamed outward and inward for exchange and stimulus. Training programs in the field and apprenticeship opportunities for Asian and African nationals could be multiplied. The dreams of Frank Laubach would then seem closer to reality. The people taught to read in his literacy campaigns have been bombarded with political propaganda and high-gloss "cheesecake." Tracts and flannelgraphs cannot compete. A new world is emerging. Its shape and tone will be largely set by the press, radio, and television. Surely it makes sense to divert some of the present fantastic global missionary expenditures on hospitals and schools into ensuring the presence of a responsible and imaginative Christian contribution within the swift development of the mass media in the next fifty years? Here is true ecumenical work to be done.

None of it will be done well without cooperation between the World Council of Churches and artists. New images, new songs, plays, films, buildings, are the living stuff that will translate intuitively what conference reports can never convey. Real artists are at work today in the mass media and in the setting of the new architecture. It is the hope of all with a love of new forms and objects that the notoriously stuffy taste of church officials will not succeed in smothering such alliances in the service of the Good News.

There has already been one sad chapter. Some of us on the staff of the World Council of Churches wanted the Council to ask Le Corbusier, the greatest architect of our time, and one of the greatest builders of all time, to design the new Geneva headquarters. It was eventually decided not to ask him, because he was thought to be hard to work with. One wonders how far this was considered a problem when Michelangelo and Bernini were at work in Rome.

Later some of us urged that there were outstanding people

available in America, Scandinavia, Germany, and Switzerland. We came up with names. The list was narrowed down to Otto Senn of Basel and Professor Otto Bartning of Germany. They were teamed together, and were good to one another, although their styles and approaches were different. Then Professor Bartning died. Successive plans from Mr. Senn were, for a variety of reasons, rejected. The whole project was tied, by advance decision, to a local Geneva building firm as executants. The firm had definite ideas about what went and what did not go in the local building trade. They had local pull and had always done the World Council's renovations and additions on the old site. They early expressed strong views about their unwillingness to work with some of the more famous and creative names on our long list of nominees. In the end, when Mr. Senn also sadly withdrew, the major responsibility fell on this firm of solid and reliable Geneva builders. Meanwhile, art by committee was practiced to a considerable extent by the World Council itself, which took due note of the judgments and preferences of a variety of influential church leaders, as to shapes, volumes, and functions. The chapel became a subject of special interest, so that a full file of the permutations and combinations proposed and dispatched will be a curiosity for future social historians.

This factual review of a situation that went through many phases should suffice to make the point that there is a right approach to creative artists which have to be discovered, and was not in this instance. Let art-lovers feel as sad as they should, so that self-criticism may lead in future to right relationships with the expert *par excellence* in the subtle art of communication, the maker of significant form.

BENT TWIGS AND ECUMENICAL BRANCHES

Walter D. Wagoner

*T*HE quest for Christian unity should have similarities to a military campaign. This is a dangerous simile in matters religious, but I would press it here. Maps need to be consulted, obstacles located, strategies devised. The wheeling, charging (and limping) denominational armies will end by shooting each other in the dark unless more deliberate and programmatic plans of attack are formulated. Charismatic "men on horseback" in the last fifty years have rallied the conscripts, raised the banners, pointed out the distant battlements. Campaigns and field maneuvers, with major engagements at Amsterdam, Evanston, and New Delhi, have been carried out. As the title of this book suggests, we now have a gathering army paused in mid-course; it must regroup, establish better organization and communications—and then march toward its next carefully chosen objectives.

Ecumenical strategy and logistics must reckon in a wise and calculating way with theological education and its centers. Ecumenical advance is hobbled sorely until and unless the schools which prepare the ordained leaders and servants of the Church are also sources of support. This chapter is a discursus on what manner of help—and of mischief—is to be found in theological education as it relates to the increase of Christian unity.

Certain German theological faculties excepted, seminaries are explicitly a part of the institutional life of the Christian Church. It would be very poor analysis to treat them as phenomena which, from the viewpoint of ecumenical advance, are exotic or *sui generis*. They are rightly to be regarded as the brain-centers of Christian church life. No major significant church movement will go far without the critical support of the seminaries. Being a part of the institutional life of Christendom, seminaries share the instinct toward order and self-preservation. Indeed, one of their major and justifiable functions is to maintain discipline and to ensure continuity.

Since the implications of Christian unity are as unsettling and terrifying to institutions as well as to individuals, seminaries are adept at dodging "ecumenical repentance." In the same breath it must be said that seminaries are also the training grounds, the theological "Etons," from whose playing fields have come numerous ecumenical leaders and adventurers: Angus Dun, Douglas Horton, John Mackay, James McCord, Walter Muelder, Liston Pope, Henry P. Van Dusen, to confine illustration to the United States. Despite leadership of this statesmanlike caliber, and in addition to the many other advances, these schools of the Church need to be under unrelenting criticism from within and without in order to make certain that their institutional strengths and functions do not smother their potential contribution to Christian unity.

The greatest danger to the ecumenical movement *is that it will be captured and domesticated by the churches*. Since Christianity cannot be defined apart from the community we call the Church, such a generalization verges on paradox. But the churches too, are always capturing and domesticating Jesus Christ. Fortunately for mankind, God will not be staked down under any of our tents. But we try. And being a part of the institutional life of the churches, the seminaries share the temptation. One of the effective ways to domesticate the ecumenical movement is to control it during the seminary years, both in the manner in which it is taught and in the attitudes toward it transmitted to theological students. The impulse to Christian unity is in real danger of being organizationally smothered by churches anxious to tidy it up, neatly agendize it, gerrymander it among parochial ward politicians. The ecumenical movement can be institutionalized in such a way that its life becomes parasitical: dependent upon the body of various church members. The domestication of Christian unity is seen, for example, in the encapsulation of Faith and Order under the Division of Studies of the World Council. The passion for unity must not be trapped and tamed on the campuses of theological education.

For all the talk about the need for a healthy balance between laity and clergy in the ecumenical movement, it is a foregone conclusion that the clergy will have the determining role in most major church movements. They are trained for it; they have the time for it. By necessity, if not by forfeiture, the clergy control budgets, agendas, and appointments. This power and this leadership role is directly shaped by the nature of theological education and preparation for ordination. Thus anyone who broods over the destiny of Christian unity finds his thoughts turning again and again to the educational centers of the church. Theological education relates directly to the advance of Christian unity in five areas: (1) the curriculum, (2) student-faculty programs, (3) international cooperation in theological education, (4) seminary structure, and (5) the ethos and attitudes inculcated by the education leading to ordination.

Curriculum

The American church historian of the distant future, looking back for significant signs of Christian advance in our time, will open his eyes at this: that from The Second Assembly of the World Council of Churches at Evanston in 1954 to the Third Assembly at New Delhi in 1961, the curriculum courses in ecumenics in American seminaries increased 800 percent!—

from some thirty courses to more than two hundred and twenty. In 1962, 85 percent of all seminaries in the American Association of Theological Schools were given academic credit for ecumenical courses and seminars.* It can be said safely that no other discipline of theological education has ever had such a dramatic growth. Indeed, where in the entire spectrum of *any type of graduate study* can there be found such a swift intrusion of a new field of study?

No one will assume that all of this attention is to be counted as pure gain for Christian unity. Some of the schools are, by denominational stance, quite unhappy with the ecumenical movement. A few will, no doubt, teach in such a fashion as to damn ecumenicity either with faint praise or loud criticism. "Iowa will go Democratic when Hell goes Methodist," runs the saying; and such are just about the odds against some seminaries displaying ecumenical sympathy. Nevertheless, the ecumenical movement is being taught by friend and foe alike. Fortunately, most of those teaching it are friendly critics and scholars.

Professor Ralph Hyslop, of Union Theological Seminary, in an address at the Biennial Convention of the American Association of the Theological Schools just prior to the Evanston Assembly had this to say:

. . . we teachers not only tend to perpetuate the divisions between the churches, but to add to them by further divisions in the subject matter of theological study . . . is it too much to expect that the theological seminaries should become vital forces in the furthering of a reformation of which the ecumenical movement is itself both a symbol and an agent?

The prospects for Christian unity are certainly affected by seminary curricula. It can now be assumed that most seminaries give such attention to the data about and interpretation of the ecumenical movement. Edinburgh, Oxford, Amsterdam, Evanston, and New Delhi are as identifiable in church history

* I wish to give credit to Professor Robert Tobias and to Walter Gallop of the Christian Theological Seminary, Indianapolis, for much of the data here quoted.

classes as Trent, Geneva, Augsburg, and Constance. Soderblom, Temple, and Visser 't Hooft are as well known as Bucer, Anselm, and Judson. No survey of missions fails to reckon with Madras or with the integration of the IMC and the WCC. On balance, the development of formal ecumenical studies in seminaries of the United States and Canada is substantial and encouraging. Within the faculties of these seminaries one can identify at least one hundred and forty teachers who give special instruction in various aspects of the ecumenical movement. More encouraging still is the fact that most of these teachers have done intensive work in the field and that their own careers have more often than not included a period of active service in one of the major ecumenical agencies.

Naturally there is much debate within seminary faculties as to how much "separate" attention should be given to ecumenics and to what extent the movements of mission, unity, and renewal are to be subsumed under the traditional disciplines of history, theology, and missions. My own conclusion is, I think, in agreement with most of those who labor in this field: that almost every regular division of the curriculum must include appropriate attention to ecumenical issues. For example, any course in nineteenth century American Church History is obligated to understand the significance of the early days of the intercollegiate student Christian movement and its effect on unity, or the Mercersburg theology and its impact on new ecclesiologies.

On the other hand, there must be room in the curriculum for specialized attention to the ecumenical movement proper. It is, after all, a fact of Christian history of as much relevance as the sixteenth century Reformation. Yale Divinity School, for example, lists under its Department of Missionary Service this course:

Ecumenical Christianity: The history of the ecumenical movement and its present organizational development; its current problems and future prospects. The major churches of the world and their attitudes toward Christian unity.

The Christian Theological Seminary at Indianapolis in its Department of Theology carries this listing:

Seminar: Faith and Order: Principal unitive and divisive factors among churches in the ecumenical movement, with particular attention to doctrinal issues.

Such courses are typical of the more than two hundred now to be found in the catalogue listings of AATS seminaries. Even when a catalogue does not carry separate listings it normally gives attention to the various aspects of the modern ecumenical reformation through classes in history, missions, and theology.

Perhaps the most impressive formal attention given to the ecumenical movement is that of The Boston University School of Theology, which has a separate Department of Ecumenics, with Dr. Nils Ehrenstrom as Chairman, and which lists eleven credit courses in the field.

The ecumenical enthusiast might well exclaim, "Who could ask for anything more?" To which the faculties of some equally large seminaries might reply that a good thing is being overdone. Theological faculties are always under pressure from various interests and pressure groups within the life of the church to have a curriculum which reflects more theology, or audiovisual education, or group dynamics, or preaching, et cetera, et cetera. It takes perspective and sanity for a faculty to balance these "lobbies." The question which the faculty committee on curricula must answer with regard to the ecumenical movement is this: "Given the resources of our faculty, budget and library, how much time and attention does the ecumenical movement merit?"

One promising curricular development at Boston and elsewhere is the growth of interseminary classes on the ecumenical movement. This writer attended a few sessions of such a group sponsored jointly by Princeton Theological Seminary, Union Theological Seminary, and Drew University School of Theology and was very much impressed with the impact of the papers and discussion.

In conclusion, curriculum offerings in ecumenics which, not many years ago, were almost bootlegged into seminaries, are now solidly established. Within the AATS there are three schools with separate departments in that field; and the wide front of course offerings is divided among the traditional disciplines of the curriculum: in Departments of Theology (37 percent), in Church History (36 percent), in Missions (20 percent), and Practical Theology (7 percent).

Faculty-Student Extracurricular Programs

What legitimate demands can Christian unity make upon the extracurricular time of the seminary community? The seminarians, like any and all graduate students, should not be diverted from their studies by activities which have little relation to education. Neither Christian unity nor good works nor parish needs should be offered as excuses for shirking the main intellectual task. But given the universal nature of the Christian Gospel, no purist attitude toward the academic life can justify the withdrawal of the seminary community from the more inclusive community of Christ. The sight of seminarians being educated in denominational isolation on their respective holy hills is not a happy one. Paraphrasing Alexander Selkirk, what type of Christian unity can be ingrained at seminaries where "from the center all round to the sea, the student sees nothing but Baptists, or eats only with Methodists, prays largely with Lutherans, communes almost exclusively with Anglicans, studies theology surrounded by Presbyterians." And this is to say nothing of the appalling shortcomings of most Protestant clergy with regard to genuine ecumenical interchange with Eastern Orthodoxy and Roman Catholicism. The attitudes formed in such encapsulated environments do not appear likely to provide that openness and flexibility and knowledge so necessary for an ecumenically minded clergy. There must be ecumenical communication and fellowship between and on the seminaries' campuses. This takes various forms: the encouragement of heady discussion and debate concerning ecclesiology,

denominational*ism,* ecclesiastic*ism,* forums for *avant garde* talk,
at the risk of wild individualism, concerning the nature of the
Christian community. This is the proper atmosphere of graduate theological study. What a bland and sterile clergy will be
produced if seminaries are expected to be only the assembly lines
for properly molded churchmen of this or that lineage! If, during the seminary years, the future minister is excited by and
engaged in various interchurch, interconfessional and ecumenical
ventures, he is never going to settle complacently for the *status
quo ante.*

In the United States and Canada, the program of the Interseminary Movement, along with the World Student Christian
Federation, is the most promising seedbed of ecumenical leadership. And if its accomplishments fall far behind its intentions,
it is largely attributable to the crippling restraints of a meager
budget.

The imaginative program of the Interseminary movement
exemplifies precisely the type of ferment so very much needed
during the formative years in the life of a minister. It is significant that this movement is affiliated with both the World
Student Christian Federation and the National Council of
Churches of Christ in the USA. It thus has a sense of responsibility to the church as an institution; the Interseminary Movement does not attempt to operate in vacuum, naïvely oblivious
of the life of the church. Dr. Robert Bilheimer, presently one of
the Associate General Secretaries of the WCC, was at one time
th Executive Secretary of the Interseminary Movement. It is
now under the energetic leadership of the Reverend Finley
Eversole, whose main effort is to make of the ISM a vigorous
counterpart of the Faith and Order Movement, a place where
"angry young seminarians" can become the conscience of the
churches and the ecumenical movement.

Beyond the program and hopes of the ISM, there are spontaneous local campus efforts: it may be a forum on the meaning
of ordination, a meeting with a staff member of the World
Council, the shaping of new worship patterns based on ecu-

menical experience, or enterprises related to refugee work and to ecumenical work camps. In 1961, the United Theological Seminary at Dayton, Ohio, sponsored a mock session of the New Delhi Assembly—a practice whose spread is commendable. The main impediment to such student ecumenical assemblies is that it is difficult to duplicate the financial and vested-interest attitudes which the postseminary year have inculcated into the actual delegates to ecumenical gatherings. It is pleasing to note, however, that the World Council, the National Council, and the Interseminary Movement are urging special seminary study groups to be formed in preparation for the 1963 meeting of Faith and Order at Montreal.

International Cooperation

Contrary to many developments in the ecumenical world, where programs often were initiated at the international level, unity movements in theological education are quite slow to form. One hopeful sign was a meeting held at New Delhi, November 20, 1961, in the course of the Third Assembly, to which some ninety theological educators came at the invitation of a steering committee looking forward to "a world consultation on theological education." Among the chief conveners were Principal Russell Chandran, President Henry P. Van Dusen, and Professor Robert Tobias. The principal question asked was, "Has the time come for the theological schools to create an instrument of worldwide consultation and collaboration?" The chief decision was to form a Continuation Committee to look into the ways and means of implementing such consultation. Obviously this was an important first meeting, but progress at this writing is slow.

Regional associations of theological educators are forming in certain areas of the world. The AATS, with 84 member seminaries is the most notable. Further, the Theological Education Fund (with backing from the International Missionary Council and from the Rockefellers' Sealantic Fund) is doing much to strengthen theological seminaries in Africa, Asia, and South America.

There is bound to emerge, despite distance and differences, that kind of cooperation and conversation among theological educators everywhere which is a necessary concomitant of growth in Christian unity. The words of President Van Dusen at the New Delhi meeting, cited above, included this sentence:

Theological education on an ecumenical basis is not new. Before the Tambaran Conference the mission bodies were deeply concerned with the fact that *the weakest single spot in the mission of the church is the training of the ministry.*

The Structure of the Seminary

Which type of seminary most adequately advances Christian unity? Is it denominational, or interdenominational or federated? Should the seminary be small and somewhat divorced from a university milieu or vice versa?

Criteria of Christian unity are not the only standards by which to evaluate the structure of a seminary; but since Christian unity is so basically an aspect of the Gospel, questions such as these have validity.

From an ecumenical viewpoint much of American seminary structure is archaic, reflecting outmoded rationales and ecclesiologies. Were we founding seminaries today, we would surely found fewer of them, and those started would not be so restrictedly denominational. Theoretically, one can conclude that the interdenominational, university-related seminary is the healthiest type of structure for theological education. This is a beguiling and partisan issue, well worth vigorous debate. On the other hand, some denominational seminaries show greater ecumenical life than some interdenominational ones. The federated type of seminary, such as the structure being formed at the Interdenominational Theological Center in Atlanta, Georgia, is in many ways the most promising experiment; but it is still too early for valid judgment.

As an Interseminary Movement study document asks, "What

are the implications for the ecumenical movement of the fact that a disproportionately large percentage of ecumenical leadership comes from the interdenominational seminaries?"

In this debate the denominational seminary is apt to present its brief in this fashion:

"The church is the real basis of ecumenicity, as of all forms of Christian life. There is no such halfway house known as interdenominational Christianity . . . there are only specific forms of the Christian community: Baptist, Lutheran, United Church of Christ, *et al.* Therefore, any ecumenicity which is realistic must spring out of denominational life. An ecumenical spirit which is not rooted in *a* church is likely to be a naïve and pseudoecumenical. For reasons of Christian unity, soberly conceived (that is, not romantically viewed), as well as for a host of practical-career-polity reasons, a denominational seminary is the best form of theological education."

In turn the interdenominational school will say:

"Denominations are at best but very incomplete manifestations of Christianity. Most of them, granting the necessity for some definite church home, are still far too much conditioned by past history and outmoded apologias. Denominations do not correspond to the real theological and intellectual issues. It is possible to establish career roots in this or that denomination without being educated within one tradition. An interdenominational community will produce an ampler and less easily satisfied interpretation of Christianity, as well as an ampler ecumenical ethos."

This type of debate, thrust and parry, can go on and on with each side hypnotized by the sounds of its own words. Presented in these divisive terms, the difference may be exaggerated more than is fair. But there are important matters here, and the time has come for responsible leaders in theological education to talk of them more openly and less defensively.

At a recent meeting of the AATS Dean Walter Muelder spoke helpfully when he said in reply to the challenge of the interdenominational viewpoint:

. . . much interdenominationalism is also preecumenical since it rests on assumptions of unity and cooperation more reminiscent of the unchurchly twenties than the era of the World Council . . . in some situations nondenominational seminaries play the ecumenical promotional theme as if church-related schools were archaic and outside the ecumenical realm. In other situations the denominational seminaries are overprotective in recruitment and defensive with respect to the alleged aggressions of nondenominational (interdenominational) institutions.

How does one see the full majesty and amplitude of the Christian faith if a theological education is focused primarily on the heritage of a particular denomination? This is still the case in more than a few seminaries. The point is not that each teacher and student is not limited by particular tradition—all of us are —but that there are no longer the easy excuses for perpetuating these stances. It is, be it admitted, rather a bore to keep making denominationalism the whipping boy. Nevertheless, the community of theological scholarship ought to be the place, above any other, where one may go to see the outlines of the Church universal, unhindered by the blinders of parochialism. An ordinand completing his theological schooling, if he goes forth having already experienced the thrilling dimensions of Christian unity, surely will be restless with any church structure that hides the vision and the reality.

The logistics of theological education makes clear what is at stake:

Denominational Seminary (related to the Church of the Brethren), has the following student enrollment:

    85 Church of Brethren
     1 Baptist
     1 Christian Catholic
     1 United Church of Christ
     1 Presbyterian

Interdenominational Seminary:

   195 Presbyterian
   112 Methodist
    83 Protestant Episcopal

52 Baptists
49 United Church of Christ
19 Disciples of Christ
13 Reformed Church in America

This is not an unusual comparison; more striking ones are available.

Such a chart proves nothing, but it does demonstrate where the greater ecumenical potentialities ordinarily will be found.

No matter how firmly one believes in the unique witness of a particular denomination; no matter how much denominations may be justified in "producing their own kind," the nature of the Christian gospel, as the ecumenical reformation testifies, no longer will permit theological education to be conducted in such an atomized fashion. Denominational seminaries do not exist in isolation, of course. They are integral parts of denominational structures, supported by denominational loyalties, recruiting their students from and feeding them back into a denominational system. But seminaries should be active in institutional self-criticism, eager for ecumenical dimensions. In order to reform the church, as it surely is being reformed under the ecumenical revolution, theological education must be, in all of its structures, more representative of the church universal.

Attitude and Ethos and Ordination

H. L. Mencken, with a caustic anticlericalism lurking behind his words, once quipped that "an ordained minister is a Christian who has attained to a higher ecclesiastical status than Jesus Christ." The old vocational vice of clericalism becomes a genuine ecumenical problem when one begins to analyze many of the frictions in interchurch relations. Officeholding, briefcase stickers, ecumenical expeditions, the desire to be a "spiritual spokesman," to be "Mr. Baptist" or "Mr. Anglican"—there is no doubt but that the plenary pomp of large ecumenical meetings and maneuverings makes for this sort of ordained halo-polishing. Any realistic analysis of strategy must take these problems into account. Relative to the total number of ministers serving the church, this stuffiness is a minor matter—most ministers, like most doctors and lawyers, do not put on airs; but in proportion to the damage which a visible minority of the pretentious and authoritarian can do to the cause of Christian unity, it becomes, indeed, a serious matter. After all, most of those attending ecumenical affairs are precisely those with the greatest personal stake in the present conformation of a denomination.

It is too easy (and if I were a seminary officer, I would resent it), to blame sin on the seminaries, even the sin of clerical feather-preening. Yet the way in which a seminary interprets the ordained office, the manner in which it shapes the ordinand obviously is crucial. It is another instance of the subtle effect that the nature of theological education has on the church and, in this context, on Christian unity. I think of several occasions of ecumenical negotiation in which, behind all the smoke screens and rationalization making much of "theological tension and exegetical differences," the real differences, as in so much of life, were threats to privilege and to the personal power of this or that leading clergyman. The trouble is that Christian unity ruthlessly asks all of us to drop our pretensions to squatters' rights on holy land. The Gospel has nothing to do with ecclesiastical preferment or denominational bandwagons. These are personal failings, and we cannot seek vicarious absolution by blaming them on the seminaries. But surely in a seminary community where there is a lack of denominational self-inflation about ordination, plus a more irenic attitude toward all other Christian confessions, there will be more promise of Christian unity.

One final point—a tender spot. Whether the theological education be in a denominational or interdenominational or federated seminary, there is no doubt but that many seminarians seek ordination and a church home in this or that denomination primarily for pragmatic, convenient, and even opportunistic reasons and *not because of significant or valid theological differ-*

ences. This merely testifies to the plain fact that in the United States, at least, and largely because of the impact of the ecumenical reformation, there is no clear relation between one's desire to enter the ordained ministry and the choice of a particular denomination. This commonplace situation is a fact of enormous significance for theological education and for ecumenicity. It is one more evidence of the make-work and artificiality behind some church differences. It means that there is a good deal of special pleading and window-dressing involved in some denominational doctrines of the ministry. It is another result of the degree to which the ecumenical earthquake of the last fifty years has fissured and sheared ecclesiologies. And it is one more reason for insisting that theological education and the preparation for the ministry be much more responsive than it is to the realities of church life and therefore to the imperatives for Christian unity.